DEDICATION

This book is dedicated to my grands, great grands, and any progeny linked (by blood or bonus) to our group of fearfully and wonderfully made people.

I wanted to tell you that this isn't to embarrass or label you. I've just found that it's so gratifying to see growth and healthy development in our family. I don't know if we're 'typical' or like the odd man out. I just know that I consider each of you a unique and beautiful display of God's grace. I look at you and I recognize not just potential and possibility. I see the beauty and the gifting you possess.

So, three things I want to pass on to you. (1).You can learn from other people's successes including mine. (2). you can learn from the mistakes and failures of others including mine. (3) You must learn to value yourself and others by (a) knowing you do not deserve to be mistreated, used, or abused in any way, and (b) You do not have the right to mistreat anyone including yourself.

I know its old school terminology but this is how I express my emotions sometimes. I think you are the bees' knees and the cat's meow. I'll love you forever and a day.

The Lord isn't nervous ...about anything. You don't have to worry either. You can trust Him.

Surviving Stupid

By O. Peterson-Brown

Books and pretty much any good reading material, that's my thing. I love words. I try to choose wisely the titles and topics I attach to any of my work. I realize I've previously been attracted to most reading material by the titles. The title either gets my attention or it does nothing at all. So, I figure other people may be drawn in the same way.

Hence, the reason for the title of this book! It may be just the thing for those who want to work through facing the past and trying to get it right. I trust it does not disappoint. If it does what it is intended to do, you'll walk away with a little more knowledge, the benefit of someone else's experience, and possibly a useful tool for life. Welcome to bits and pieces of a fellow traveler on this journey called life. Not just any life though. This is the life we live as imperfect human beings learning to depend on the unadulterated (though often misunderstood) Word of Almighty God.

Ephesians 5:1 Therefore be imitators of God [copy Him and follow His example], as well-beloved children [imitate their father]. 2 And walk in love, [esteeming and delighting in one another] as Christ loved us and gave Himself up for us, a [a] slain offering and sacrifice to God [for you, so that it became] a sweet fragrance [AMP].

Should you find it worth while, please pass it on to someone else who might be helped by the content.

If you don't, pass it on anyway. You never know where other people are in their walk. This may be the very thing to educate and encourage them to keep going no matter how horribly they've messed up. It was things like this that helped me when I was searching.

Transparency and the truth I found in God's Word brought me such freedom and clarity. I grew in leaps and bounds once I discovered the fact that love never fails. True love surpasses our emotional roller coasters on steroids. God's love is beyond the superficial, ever changing, and conditional love we've lived with amongst ourselves.

The solution to our dilemma we've been saddled with isn't really a dilemma at all. We've worried over getting it right, being loved, being treated well or even fairly. Then God offers something we never expected: Agape - His unconditional, pure, undiluted love for mankind.

What's Inside?

Pull Over. Let's Talk About That

This section is designed to encourage and challenge you to remember how you made decisions in the past; hopefully prepare you for your next chapter; and help you work on daily life choices in being present and accountable today. Change is inevitable but the direction of that change is often dictated by perspective.

George Santayana is credited with the famous **quote**, *"Those who do not remember the past are condemned to repeat it."*

I KNOW WHAT I

WAS FEELING, BUT

WHAT WAS I

THINKING??

WHAT WAS I THINKING?

I know what I was feeling but **WHAT WAS I THINKING?**

Some days, I have moments where I just go to the wall with God. I look back over my life and that's what I say. What in the world was I thinking? The same thing some of you are thinking right now and the same thing so many of you have thought in the past.

I've got this.
It won't happen to me.
I'm smarter than that.
There's no way I'm going down that road.
They just didn't know how to handle it.
She simply didn't know how to side step that one. I'll do better.

I'm in awe of how God allowed me to survive the crazy years and utter foolishness of my youth.

I've done many foolish things. Most of that foolishness is in my past, but why should you listen to me?

Well, let's try this on for size: *I SURVIVED IT AND I DON'T RECOMMEND THAT ROUTE TO YOU! IT WAS ABSOLUTELY HORRIBLE AND FOR MOST OF THAT TIME I WAS MISERABLE. WHAT'S WORSE IS THAT I TOOK INNOCENT LIVES INTO THAT FOOLISHNESS AND CRAZINESS WITH ME! I MADE IT THROUGH BUT IT WAS AN INSANELY EXPENSIVE JOURNEY!*

The word 'through' is described as: moving in one side and out of the other side of (an opening, channel, or location).

"Stepping boldly through the doorway"

Synonyms: into and out of, to the other side of, to the far side of, from one side to the other of

We drove through the tunnel. As soon as we opened the gate they came streaming through.

From one end to the other.

Verb: endure, experience, suffer, survive, undergo, withstand, bear, brave, support, swallow, tolerate

Genesis 4:3, 8, 14; Genesis 6:1; Genesis 7:10; 1 Kings 18:1; Matthew 7:28; Matthew 9:10; Matthew 19:1; Luke 2:1 + numerous other places in scripture is the phrase:
'It came to pass or *AND it came to pass*.' And it came to pass occurs 396 times in the KJV (or 453 times if the word 'and' is missing).

That's what I am now receiving in my life as a sure fire way to look at every season, every incident, every occurrence, and time I've approached and gone *THROUGH*. It came to pass.

In George Foreman's book, God in My Corner – A Spiritual Memoir, in the section entitled: Storms Don't Last, he mentions this:

Someone asked an elderly woman her favorite Scripture. She replied, "And it came to pass." The response to her was – But that doesn't mean anything. She said, "Yes it does. I know that whenever a trial comes, it doesn't come to stay; it comes - to pass. It's not going to be around forever."

Though her understanding of it may have been a bit different, she was definitely headed in the right direction for gaining the freedom and the truth that every single one of us needs.

Consider the realms and seasons that each of us deals with at some point in our lives:

Our bodies – came to pass.
The teen years – came to pass.
School attendance –came to pass.
Our jobs/careers – came to pass.
Seasons of our lives – came to pass.
Parenting toddlers, teens, adult children – came to pass.
Our issues – came to pass.
Our victories – came to pass.
Our friends, families, words, foolishness, knowledge, courage, cowardice, energy, station in life, etc. – All of these came to move on, they happened, they ***came to pass.***

WE HAVE AN EXPIRATION DATE

WE HAVE AN EXPIRATION DATE!

Let me make it even clearer – *they came into being and they also have an expiration date! None of what we deal with, what we experience, or what we see is permanent. What we have here is all temporary. WE HAVE AN EXPIRATION DATE!*

I've been known to say to loved ones and family members, 'you don't have to experience everything yourself to gain wisdom or knowledge'. Those on the fast track in this life for positive things often learn to use other peoples' life experiences to bypass (avoid) and even expedite some things. We're all books ripe with fruit for the reading/picking if the reader would pay attention. No matter how smart you are (we are), there is someone who knows more or someone who has a different vantage point. Take **AD**vantage of that person's experience.

Though it came into being and into existence, according to the Word of God, basically if we can see it then it is temporary.

2 Corinthians 4:16-18 New International Version (NIV)

16 Therefore we do not lose heart. Though outwardly we are wasting away, yet
inwardly we are being renewed day by day. 17 For our light and momentary troubles are
achieving for us an eternal glory that far outweighs them all. 18 So we fix our eyes not on
what is seen, but on what is unseen, since what is seen is temporary, but what is unseen
is eternal.

If we would but recognize the Truth He wants us to get. That TRUTH is that the permanent side of our lives is the spiritual and we will all either accept or reject it.

He – God – has made provision for the Spiritual side of us as the part that will continue even when these bodies no longer function. The natural realm of this life is temporary and the Spiritual side, the spiritual realm, continues once the natural side is done and is no more.

And it came to pass.... I'm just passing through. This too will pass. There used to be an acronym that I enjoyed a lot...PUSH – Pray Until Something Happens. It isn't magic. It is a principle of God. John 15:7

Proverbs 18:21 Death and life are in the power of the tongue; and they that love it shall eat the fruit thereof.

Watch your words because they do have power. We will behave based on what we think and believe.

1. Hear it
2. Think it
3. Say it
4. Believe it
5. Do it/Be it

That's the spiritual creating and controlling the natural, the stuff we think turns into words. We say the words. We believe those words. We act on those words. We become what we say. We receive what we say.

My natural/physical life? It didn't come to stay, at least not as it is at this moment. I'm not where I was 10 years ago. I'm not where I will be in 10 years from right now. I don't have visions of grandeur but I believe that there is a progression as I speak the rich Word of God over my life. I am aware that even as I speak the Word over our children and our entire bloodline, there are things happening that we cannot see in the natural at this moment. I am cooperating with God as I learn more and more about Him and His desires, His plans for me. When I pray for our kids, I realize they have free will and that prayer is not magic. However, as I continue to learn and understand what the Word says, I am realizing that I can't pray one way and then go into murmuring and complaining conversations. *I can't afford to practice prayer and practice fear and worry at the same time!*

James 1:8 King James Version (KJV)

8 A double minded man is unstable in all his ways.

So, if I see something happening that isn't in line with the way I'm praying, I need to be sure that I rehearse the direction of prayer I desire and not rehearse the problem.

It seems to me that if I pray one thing and then say another in my conversation, I'm sabotaging what my true desires are.

I have the advantage of a past. I'm on the other side of my past. It didn't come to stay. Even in my foolishness, the detours, and rebellion, it is evident that God never left my side. He never had to go into panic mode or push the panic button. He always knew that I would come to my right mind (The Mind of Christ).

THROUGH IT ALL

Through it All

He heard every scream and saw (collected) every tear. He knew when they were just emotional cries because I didn't want to hurt and I was in the moment...*In my feelings.*

He also knew when the genuine screams and cries for His intervention came and the resolve was there for change. He knew that my tears were not only real but I was ready to be seriously faithful and there would finally be no turning back. He knew exactly what it would take for me to do an about-face, my personal 180. He knew what I would have to **GO THROUGH** to get to this place, the other side. He knew that because of my makeup, my history, and my state of mind that I had to face ME and the reality of my own life before I was ready to get to the other side.

God has been good to me. He's real. He loves me. He will never leave or forsake me. He will get me to the other side. He will get me ***THROUGH*** it all and SAFELY ***TO*** the other side.

The song, 'Through it All' (Andre Crouch 2003):

> Through it all.
> THROUGH it all.
> I've learned to trust in Jesus.
> I've learned to trust in God.
> Through it all.
> Through it all.
> I've learned to depend upon His Word.

Honestly, I have been in some situations where I found myself headed to work in a car that was operating on a wing and a prayer. It was seriously on its last legs but I needed to get to work so I drove it.

During that 30 minute drive, I found myself screaming at the top of my lungs as I traveled because I was in a self-made very desperate situation. I was in a horrible, miserable, and abusive relationship that I had no business in because '*I knew better.*' I was in it because I'd left another one where *I had a right to leave and divorce him*. To be perfectly honest, I was afraid that if I didn't go into this relationship (which I didn't know for sure at the time it would be abusive), I'd end up back in the other one where adultery and outside children were involved.

I cried out to God and begged Him to help me. I had been in so many bad relationships and situations. I never thought I'd have to endure something like this. Yet, there I was.

I'd heard the voice of God in many different ways before. I knew when He was trying to get a message to me. I had ignored those messages when they didn't say what I wanted to hear. *That was disobedience.*

I suffered the consequences of that disobedience. You don't ignore God's Word, His warnings, and His wisdom and expect there to be no consequences. I knew that but I was driven by so many foolish things, including my ever changing, unpredictable, and unreliable emotions.

I was dealing with major emotions. There was pride, obligation, fear, embarrassment, guilt, anger, a desire for revenge, bitterness, naiveté, shame, and a plethora of other emotions out of control.

I allowed myself to be swayed by the flood of emotions that came when I left my (soon to be) ex-husband and took on a lover. I later recognized that 'lover' for who and what he really was. He was a well-placed messenger/employee of Satan. He knew his job and assignment better than many Christians know theirs. My level of discernment at the time was particularly low. Strangely enough, God used him as a tool to wake me up!

Once I admitted how wrong I was, God sent one of His servants, a woman of God, by to confirm my suspicions about this current relationship. Still, pride, a sense of obligation, fear, embarrassment and the rest took over.

You may be able to identify with where I was at the time. I knew it was unhealthy to go back into the relationship with my ex. He not only cheated on me but by that time, he had fathered a number of other children outside of our marriage. I didn't think I had the ability to take care of my kids alone. I'd heard it enough times and somehow, I believed it. As strange as that might seem, I had already been taking care of me, the kids, and the ex! Somehow, my brain must have been on pause because I didn't connect the dots. Besides, I didn't think I was strong enough to say 'no' to him. I knew my emotional attachment to him wasn't over and he wanted to come back.

Friends, this was more than conflicted emotions. I was in deep, deep trouble and didn't know of a single human being I could go to for help. Instead of laying out before God and waiting for an answer and a solution for my dilemma, I dove head first into the absolute worst relationship I had ever been in.

The cost was great.

I wish I could say this was the only time I ever made bad decisions about relationships. I wish I could say that up to that point, I'd been pretty smart but that would not be the truth.

In fact, all of my relationships prior to that had been just as empty and just as foolish. By the grace of God I came out of those fires but I was badly burned and I was not alone.

My babies were wounded as well.

THE NAMES HAVE BEEN CHANGED TO PROTECT THE GUILTY

-OR-

GOD AND HIS GENEROUS GRACE

The Names Have Been Changed to Protect the Guilty
OR
God and His Generous Grace

The title of this book is a testament to the power of Almighty God and His Generous Grace. That is the only thing that helped me to survive stupid or foolish behavior. Not pretty words or titles but when you think about it, that's what it was.

I'm not one to beat a dead horse, so to speak (as in rehearsing or dwelling on the mistakes and bad moves I've made). Yet, I believe it's important to revisit history in an effort to avoid unwanted, undesired repeat performances. Revealing our weaknesses or sin has the potential to help someone else avoid similar or worse disasters.

Without exercising wisdom, there are some things that you just might not survive. Thank God, I survived. However, please believe me, there was a lot of fallout because there is such a thing as the domino effect. It isn't pretty.

Survive: live, endure, continue, last, outlive, outlast, stay alive, etc.

So, what you're getting here is an opportunity to learn from someone who has been in the trenches. I know what can happen if we're not alert and aware ('woke' in today's vernacular). I've also come to understand this: The enemy of our souls doesn't care how we go out as long as we become ineffective as useful vessels and witnesses in the Body of Christ.

Stupid: unwise, senseless, ill-advised, imprudent, thoughtless, rash, irresponsible, reckless, heedless; unintelligent, dim, thick, dense, slow, dull, brainless, dim-witted, obtuse, witless.

How did I survive such horrific relationships and circumstances? All I can really tell you **again** is that God determined I would live and I did. If you look at where I was, you'll immediately know that I should have died a long time ago. ***BUT GOD!***

What makes a woman go into something that dangerous and damaging? What cause or reason could she have to subject herself *and her children* to degradation and potential danger of such monumental degrees?

Desperation. There is a portion of scripture that has always been somewhere on my radar to gain better understanding and today I'll share what I believe it means.

Isaiah 4:1"And in that day seven women shall take hold of one man, saying, We will eat our own bread, and wear our own apparel; only let us be called by thy name; to take away our reproach."

The chapters prior to that explain the 7:1 ratio. The cultural standards of that day (in that place) also make it clearer as to how they got there. Bottom line, there was a shortage of men and the women were desperate to do whatever it took to be linked to a man, any man, and produce children – especially boys. The normal role of the male to provide for women and family was excused (overlooked) in order to fulfil what was considered more important…That was to be called by a man's name… to belong to someone…even being fully aware that it would be part time, at best.

To be with a man was considered more important than the normal role he would have taken – provider, protector, guardian- because the women were desperate. To have a pair of thighs, a warm body next to them in bed had become more important than dignity and holiness. They were sucked in and influenced by the immoral codes and mores (ethics, behaviors, morals, standards, values, and customs) of their surroundings.

They had been warned. They didn't take heed. They got the consequences they'd been warned about. They fell into ways and habits designed to suck the life out of them. God is not playing. This stuff is real.

Desperate times. Desperate measures. Unwanted consequences. This was the case both then and now.

Consider where we are today. Consider where I was when I was in that same frame of mind.

Domestic violence facts from 2017:

- On an average, 24 people per minute are survivors of rape, physical violence or stalking by an intimate partner in the United States
- More than 12 million women and men over the course of a year
- 1 million women reported being raped in a year and over 6 million women and men were victims of stalking in a year
- Intimate partner violence alone affects more than 12 million people each year

    - Intimate partner violence is defined as any physical or sexual violence, stalking, and psychological aggression by a current or former intimate partner. And a 'partner' can be a boyfriend or girlfriend, dating partner, sexual partner, or spouse – and it doesn't have to be someone that you were sexually intimate with
        - Source: The CDC's National Intimate Partner and Sexual Violence Survey
- Nearly 1 in 4 women and 1 in 7 men have experienced severe physical violence by an intimate partner in their lifetime
- Both men and women can be survivors of domestic violence. The CDC defines severe physical violence as including being hurt by pulling hair, being hit with something hard, being kicked, being slammed, choking or suffocating, being beaten, being burned, or any violence using a gun or knife
- The presence of a gun in domestic violence situations increases the risk of homicide for women by 500%
- According to the FBI's Supplementary Homicide Report, domestic violence is also considered a gun violence issue, because 53% of women murdered with guns in the U.S. in 2011 were killed by intimate partners or family members. (See 2003 study on 220 intimate partner femicide victims and 343 abused women).
- Nearly half of all women and men in the United States will experience psychological aggression by an intimate partner in their lifetime.

These are just a few statistics showing where we've been, where we are, and most likely where this nation is headed.

"Ladies and gentlemen: the story you are about to hear is true. Only the ***names have been changed*** *to protect the innocent."* These words were used as a narrative at the beginning of what started out as a radio series "Dragnet". Over time, the show was carried on to television. I found it appropriate for this section because in this case, guilty people should have been exposed but they were not. What a terrible thing to have innocent people hurt and guilty ones protected, don't you think?

Take a look, if you will, at a few observations in the verbiage wherein this information is concerned.

The word, **spouse**, does show up but for the most part **'intimate partner'** is used. Now, I know that getting married doesn't preclude or rule out domestic violence. I'm also aware that sin is the cause and at the core of all outrageous and egregious acts and mentalities.

To explore my reason for going in this direction, ask yourself how many words or phrases have changed or added to their meanings over time. For instance, the word '**adultery**' has been replaced by the word **'affair'** in cases of cheating spouses.
Adultery: infidelity, disloyalty, falseness, treachery, betrayal, deceitfulness, faithlessness.

Affair: matter, issue, concern, business, situation, event, thing.

Notice the difference? An **affair** is more palatable in this culture. **Adultery** is almost slander now. It's downright offensive! Affair is a much softer and acceptable word. In fact, it's almost brushed aside because it doesn't have the look, the sound, or the true severity of what took place. In other words, it's acceptable because we've toned it down. We've watered it down because *no one (the guilty party) wants to admit they've sinned!*

Whore: ('ho' or 'hoe' in urban vernacular) A prostitute, sell one's body, sell oneself, be on the streets; a prostitute; escort.

Spouse abuse, Domestic abuse; Intimate partner violence, beat down, physical attack, slap, hit, beat, strangle, murder, etc. What do all of these words and phrases have in common? Someone's personal space was not only invaded but they were somehow violated or attacked, and damaged. Someone was harmed.

I started out talking about my attitudes and mindsets during turbulent times. I thought I had it all together until I discovered that I didn't. I mentioned how damaging it was for me and many of the people that I love. (See my earlier book "Hit Me, Kick Me, Hit Me Again")

I THOUGHT I HAD IT ALL TOGETHER! (Until I Discovered I Didn't.)

I Thought I Had It All Together! (Until I Discovered I Didn't.)

The abuse started long before I had a say in the matter. My confusion and distress began when I was a child.

Male family members and 'friends of the family' violated something sacred. When I should have been safe, I was not. Where I should have been protected, I was not. Where I should have been loved, cherished, and held in high regard, I was not. I know that I'm not alone in this. There are many of you (or someone you know) who have experienced the same or very similar things.

Inappropriate touching is a no-no and unacceptable at any age, but to have that done to me at 5 or 6 years old? Capital punishment sounded good to me for years.

It was kept in the family. I overhead hushed conversations and snatches of references involving the person(s) every now and then but nothing official was ever done about it. There were threats made to and about the offender but that was it. Once discovered, I was never left in their presence or care again and that was a good thing. Still, it just seemed so unfair and unfinished. It actually caused me to think that it (the inappropriate behavior) was somehow my fault. I don't remember ever voicing it, but I thought that I had done something to entice them. That incident began the rollercoaster ride and the downward spiral into my years of rebellion and trying to find myself. Trying to be accepted, affirmed, and approved of.

Of Course there was the issue of the DMIA (Dad Missing In Action). You can see more on that subject in another one of my books: ('Male Presents, Male Presence'.)

Though I survived that one and a few others after that, I walked in a state of confusion and limbo which lasted for a very long time. Looking back, I now realize that so many of my moves were foolish to the point of bordering on *stupid*.

I suppose that's why it bothers me so much that I could have overlooked some of the same things when raising my girls. It was all a plot to destroy not just me but them as well.

In cases of adults/parents who fail to protect, even though they might suspect something is wrong, terribly wrong, I'd venture saying their radars work but the gas pedal is faulty.

So, how many ways can I say "I'm sorry"? This can be the sin of commission or omission.

Commission would be the one where I did something like inviting someone into my home (to live) that I know nothing about. I don't know their history, their habits, beliefs, or any personal things that would give me a sense of peace about them. No background check, no checking with other people who might know them. Even if I checked, I ignore the facts and still leave that person in place and my people uncovered.

The sin of omission would be ignoring the signs completely. Failure to act on what even appears to be danger to my vulnerable loved ones is called Failure To Protect; Doing nothing in defense of another or to prevent abuse. Abuse takes on many forms: Physically, mentally, financially, emotionally and spiritually. It affects us in such devastatingly harmful ways. We have to wake up and realize that there is an enemy out there. He doesn't mind using those closest to us to take us out. If we don't wake up, we'll find ourselves walking in mine fields and inviting Molotov cocktails into our homes.

Please hear me when I say, some things are preventable. We put our heads in the sand, look the other way, fear airing our dirty laundry, and don't do things differently. That opens the door for hell to have its way and our babies will continue to pay the price for our stupidity.

I read something a little while ago and it was a plea to women. It went something like this: When there is a choice to be made between protecting your children or your boyfriend, please protect your children, not your boyfriend.

I say the same: It is possible that he's not trustworthy. Be particular and intentional about whom you select/allow to be around your kids. If you do realize or even suspect that something is not right with him (or her), for heaven's sake, please choose to protect that child!

Think about this; just go with me for a moment here. Do you have any idea as to how difficult it is to repair a person who is broken, damaged, and betrayed by someone they should have been able to trust? What if that person whom you have chosen to be in the same circle as you and your child(ren) turns out to be a predator who was not trustworthy? All of this happens when the research, caution, discernment, and carefulness isn't in place. This happens when we don't pray and wait for God to respond. This happens when we don't exercise holy discernment and wisdom. This happens whenever we run head long and rough shod over God's counsel.

It happens when we rush into a relationship out of desperation. All of this misery comes just to give you, Mom, a male body that probably doesn't even satisfy your basic desires (just being real)and certainly very few (if any) of your needs.

If you see or think you see a red flag, pay attention. Make the adjustments you need to. Then use the gas pedal and get away from that person. Do you get an uneasy feeling in the midst of your stomach when you think about them? A gnawing thought that just won't go away? In today's age of advanced technology, information can be obtained in a matter of seconds. Go ahead and do a background check. If they did it before, it could happen again. Trust your gut (but for sure the Spirit of God) and not your emotions and certainly not your loins!

WHERE ARE THE SMART WOMEN?

Where Are The Smart Women?

We've got smart phones, smart homes, smart cars, and smart everything else. When do we become smart women? Smart Moms? Smart protectors? Smart nurturers? How does technology get beyond the smart people who invent and use the devices?

How do you cope with that? Even years down the road, how do you justify any of it? If you don't know Jesus, I suggest you get to know Him soon. We can often explain it but there is no justification. My heart breaks from one incident to the next as I hear of women doing the exact same things that I did. There has to be someone out there who will draw the line.

Even then, there's no 'recall' on whatever has already happened to you or your babies. That ship has sailed but there is hope for the future. The redeeming factor in it is that you know that you're forgiven by God and hopefully, by the kids as well.

There's no guarantee as to whether the kids will, though. I've actually known people who took anger, hatred, bitterness, and unforgiveness to their graves. I'm not saying unforgiveness is excused, or that it's right, and certainly God doesn't overlook it, but it does happen.

What I don't want to do is to leave you with the fear of all men. All men are not equal and you should be aware of that. All men (and women) are born into sin and yes, are capable of heinous things but not all have the desire or the propensity to damage or destroy children. Contrary to what I heard most of my adolescent years and into adulthood: All Men Are Not Dogs.

Mistakes have the potential to help us become better people. The degree to which that potential is released depends on how we behave after those mistakes are made. Mistakes, sins, or weights all have the tendency to do great harm if not properly dealt with...recognition, exposure, repentance, forgiveness.

Understand the difference between guilt & shame...

1. Admit you messed up

2. Then, own your mistakes
    A. Don't go with: "**if** I hurt, **if** I did..."
    B. Be specific
    C. Apologize to anyone you have hurt

D. Give those whom you've wronged the space and time to process

Guilt: responsibility for wrongdoing or failure
Shame: the susceptibility to such emotion; a condition of humiliating disgrace or disrepute'; something that brings censure or reproach, also something to be regretted, overwhelming emotion of regret

Condemnation – No hope, gives up

Conviction – acknowledges responsibility, brings repentance with hope

FIND HEALING FOR YOURSELF

Find Healing For Yourself

Begin to find healing for yourself.

1. Write out an apology
   a. Explore the offence for truth
   b. Remember that the person offended may or may not be correct in their thinking, but they perceive it as true
   c. Do not be condescending toward them no matter what you discover or know to be the truth
2. Know that this error, incident, or situation doesn't define you
3. You rarely heal in a punitive environment
4. Learn from your mistakes
5. What's the point of feeling guilty if it doesn't change how you'll respond in the future?
6. Take care of yourself, spiritually, mentally, & physically.

- Carrying guilt and shame too long can cause distance in our relationships.
- Carried even longer, it can begin to alter our perception of ourselves
- This takes a significant toll on our confidence, spiritual, mental and physical health
- That's why it's important to apologize and forgive yourself as soon as possible
- Muscle tension, headaches, GI (gastrointestinal) issues, lack of focus and concentration, are all possible symptoms of unforgiveness, unconfessed sin, guilt and shame

    - Move your body
    - practice intentional breathing
    - eat healthy, even if you feel the inclination to punish yourself
    - Don't give up and don't give in
    - Find something to thank God for every single day throughout the day and at day's end
        - Eyesight
        - Hearing
        - Taste
        - Smell
        - Feeling sensitivity
        - Emotions
        - Breathing
        - Mobility
        - Job
        - Finances

- Transportation
- Parents
- Spouse
- Children
- Food
- Clothes
- Stability
- Cognizance
- Opportunity
- 2 hands
- 10 toes
- Kidneys
- Hair
- Skin
- A beating heart
- LIFE
- Being able to think and reason
- Be creative in being thankful

Be patient…

You can't rush your own feelings, and you certainly can't make anyone else move faster in their emotions, either.

Sometimes we overshoot and flog ourselves because of what we've done to others and ourselves. What good does that accomplish?

BE AT PEACE WITH YOURSELF AND WITH GOD

Be At Peace With Yourself and With God

Once you realize you have actually done all you could possibly do to make amends, accept that and be at peace with yourself and with God.

Try accepting that there's nothing else you can do to resolve the issue. Cease and desist your worrying.

Of course, your feelings may still be there tomorrow, but at least they won't have ruined your entire day or the rest of your life.

Don't try to change other people...

If you've apologized to the people you hurt, and begun the process of forgiving yourself, it's possible that you'll feel embarrassed by your previous actions/behavior—if only because you're still concerned with how other people feel about you.

Please realize that other people's opinions only hold so much weight, and their opinions are rarely part of the solution.

Practice what you preach.

Everyone makes mistakes—whether they're accidents or bad judgement calls. Anyone not willing to admit that is either walking blind, walking in deceit, or they're bald faced liars.

Learn to process feelings of guilt. Reject those feelings of shame.

That will prevent reacting in a way we might regret, or worse, continuing to *feel bad*, and wallowing in self-pity for something we can't change. Practice doing that same thing for other people. Don't shame people who've wronged you, & truly grant them forgiveness... The first and most important part of forgiveness is to make the decision to forgive. Work on the emotions as time and prayer go on.

This might be the hardest part. Often when we feel embarrassed and guilty about our actions, we want everything to be back to normal (especially if we've hurt people). You can't rush your own feelings, and you certainly can't make anyone else move faster in their emotions. We cannot dictate to others how long they should grieve or how long it takes them to release feelings about what happened to them. We're individually and ultimately responsible for ourselves. We each have to face it and process it. No matter how anyone else sees it or what they think, God has the final say and He will judge.

Rev 12:9And the great dragon was hurled down—that ancient serpent called the devil and Satan, the deceiver of the whole world. He was hurled to the earth, and his angels with him. 10And I heard a loud voice in heaven, saying: "Now have come the salvation and the power and the kingdom of our God, and the authority of His Christ. For the accuser of our brothers has been thrown down, he who accuses them day and night before our God. 11They have conquered him by the blood of the Lamb and by the word of their testimony. And they did not love their lives so as to shy away from death.

Feelings and emotions **are real** but **are they the right tools** to depend on for correct moves and measures to take?

Only going to the doctor when sick? Like that with God? ER physician? ER God?

Hmmmmm…

WALKING AWAY

Walking Away

I had walked away from an adulterous marriage and that was a move I had every right to make. The problem was that I had walked out on God and His calling on my life. To add insult to injury, I had taken my children with me into something that was like a never ending scene from a horror movie except it was real.

1. Walking away from God is always a mistake no matter what the reason.
2. My actions were purely emotional and completely selfish.
3. I did not put my children's welfare first and their well-being was at risk.
4. I walked into a situation where I had not considered the consequences of my sin.
5. I ignored a word of warning because I wanted to 'make it right' on my own.
6. Ignoring the warning was an indication of my pride and foolishness.
7. God's love, mercy, and grace are the only reasons I'm alive to tell this story.

The incidents of violence continued and I became desperate to get out but I didn't know how. During that time (the 80's), it was not uncommon for law enforcement to look on domestic violence as not so serious. There was this chase scene where I had the girls with me and I was speeding down back roads to avoid another violent encounter. After literally dragging him alongside my car (he was trying to open the car door on the driver's side to pull me out), he finally fell off and got into his vehicle and came after us. I saw two policemen at a gas station and I swerved in, told them what was happening and asked for their help. They told me they didn't get into family squabbles and the best they could do was take him away from the house for a few hours to let him cool off. That taught me three things: 1) I could not depend on any help from law enforcement; 2) this man was determined to kill me if he could because he was out of control; 3) if God didn't come to my rescue, I was a dead woman. I was beyond scared or fearful. I was terrified. I knew that my actions had been wrong and I cried out to God for help. I needed a solution and it wasn't something I could just conjure up or come up with on my own. I took a serious look at what I had done and I genuinely repented. I was in a situation that called for Power beyond me. I wasn't just sorry for the mess I was in. I was sorry that I had turned away from God. This was no longer business as usual with a casual occasional prayer. My life and my children's futures depended on my next move and I knew it.

I found myself screaming and crying out to God to and from work. I couldn't do it when he was at home because he had to feel in control. My visits to any church were controlled and either approved or denied by him. Yet whenever I was home alone, I did the same thing and I began to devour and study the Word on a regular basis. Then I began to experience a peace I hadn't felt since I got myself into this relationship. It didn't stop the violence but it gave me a calmness that I can't explain. I didn't know how but I knew that God was going to work this out for me. I knew that I was forgiven, loved, and treasured.

It took some time but God delivered me out of the hands of my abuser. The damage was great but the healing has been even greater. My outlook on domestic violence has since become not only sincere but actually prepared me for ministry to others. Do I still struggle because of it sometimes? Indeed, I do. Has it left scars and wounds that are real and visible? Yes. The symptoms sometimes feel like the description for people with PTSD (Post Traumatic Stress Disorder) a mental health condition that can occur after various kinds of trauma. Back then, I didn't know what it was. I just knew that I wasn't fully functional as I needed to be. I glossed over some things and limped along until God began to peel back the layers of pain. Things I needed to face and deal with were revealed and handled one by one. The first one was learning how to forgive myself. It wasn't overnight and there are days even now that I have to dive into the Word for relief and reminders of what God has done. Over thirty years later, I still sometimes need to be reassured and have it reinforced that it really is over.

Again, I only found rest when I allowed God to take me through the process, His process, of healing and recovery.

YES, I AM A SURVIVOR

Yes, I Am a Survivor

Becoming a survivor of domestic violence and abuse had much to do with appetite. In the throes of the abuse, I developed a hunger for God and His Word. I read and studied voraciously. I began to feel stronger. My thirst for holiness and my desire to help other people became my daily quest. It is very easy to allow the emotional side of healing to override the promptings and warnings of the Holy Spirit. In my excitement and the joy of being free, although I was sincere, I was leaving some things undone.

My relationship with the kids suffered. My first order of business along with getting healthy should have been to make amends and repairs between us. I didn't know how to do that. To be perfectly honest, I was afraid of being rejected. I tried to fix things from time to time but too much time had passed and too much had happened to get back what I so desired. Don't get me wrong. They love me and I definitely love them but when I should have been protecting them, I was seeking 'happiness' for myself. You see, some things are taught and some things are caught. We learn by the words we hear and by the examples we see. No matter what my words were, I exemplified selfishness and a lack of good parenting in my actions. It was a hard thing to accept but I modeled the exact opposite of the very things I was telling them.

I didn't intend to but I my behavior was like a blaring horn or a super nova. Maybe it became a beacon of confusion. Saying one thing and then doing another? I had betrayed them and shirked my responsibilities as a mother. Dealing with the guilt, regret and every other thing that comes with it has been hard but that's on me and comes as another consequence of disobedience to Jesus Christ. I have learned that the condemnation only comes from my enemy, Satan. So, as a seasoned Christian, I plow through with prayer because I know that I'm forgiven and those sins are under the Blood of Jesus. When the waves come and regret tries to take me under, I go back to the Word for confirmation and consolation. It takes courage and determination but it has to be intentional and takes a conscious effort. I can't wallow in self-pity or have a pity party every time Satan brings condemnation. I have had to do what every serious Child of God has to do: Stay in the Word, Stand on the Word, and Walk in the Word.

I tried to make up for my disobedience and the fallout by throwing myself into 'ministry' to others, being at church every time the doors opened.

While I did that, my babies did not have a mom. My kids needed me to be present, attentive, open and honest with them. It isn't or shouldn't be a matter of one or the other. Sometimes it's a simple matter of priority and balance. Yes, I needed to be in church but I also needed to spend quality time with my children. I needed to know them and they needed to know me. The flaw was that I didn't realize the balance I needed with the girls. Work and church became my 'go to' places instead of God becoming my 'Go To' Person.

You and I are not going to be able to do a 'recall' on those years. What I'd love to have is a respectful and honoring friendship between me and my children. If that doesn't happen, I'll still do everything I hear God saying I should to make the effort.

Sometimes, I recognize there's been too much damage from the storms. I understand that. That doesn't stop me from seeking God on His counsel for restoration and healing. So, in the spirit of keeping hope alive, I still say "BUT GOD". He is alive and able to do more than I could ask, think or imagine. He is the GOD OF HOPE, remember? *Romans 15:13* **Now** *the God of hope fill you with all joy and peace in believing, that ye may abound in hope, through the power of the Holy Ghost.; Ephesians 3:20 Now unto Him that is able to do exceeding abundantly above all that we ask or think, according to the power that worketh in us, 21 Unto him be glory in the church by Christ Jesus throughout all ages, world without end. Amen.*

HOW SOON DOES IT BEGIN?

How Soon Does It Begin?

The patterns of abuse and accepting abuse began very early in my childhood. In the world I grew up in, abuse was pretty much the norm. From my vantage point, two words seemed to be interchangeable: **love**/**violence**. When a man **loved** a woman, he was jealous, therefore he beat her to be sure he kept her in line and kept her as his own. When a woman **loved** a man, if he cheated on her, she went after the person he was cheating with and oftentimes she'd go after him as well. It was not a strange thing to hear bodies thudding against walls in the middle of the night because people were ***'in love'***. Sometimes, the fights would involve knives, guns, blood spilled and lives lost because of 'love'. I still have vivid memories of running during the night, wet grass catching my ankles and legs, accompanied by the urgent fear of being caught if we didn't hurry. You see, because we were being chased by someone who **loved** Momma, we had to move quickly and be smart about it. The same thing was happening with most of our neighbors. Screams and expletives up and down the alley (street) could be heard and dramatic scenes observed like clockwork. Although, this happened mostly on the weekends when the drinking (alcohol) was at its height, it wasn't restricted to that time slot. Some of us kids knew to huddle together and stay out of the way from Friday quitting time until late Sunday night because the adults were 'having fun'. They were violently **'in love'**.

During high school, I miraculously managed to escape the drama of that kind of love (for the most part) but I came dangerously close. It was in my last year of high school that I fell in love with a guy about 10 years my senior. He was the first one to personally introduce me to domestic violence and abuse. I experienced things that I should have used as references of what not to do. I should have retained the information but I didn't because I was in ***love***! He ***loved*** me. So, let's add my naiveté, the age difference, his insecurities, and his history. The consequences would have to be disaster. Yes, he proved his love with jealousy and violence. After that, my chances for healthy relationships were greatly reduced.

Somewhere prior to that time, I was diagnosed as manic depressive. The term is now called bipolar disorder and it lingered for 25 years. That depression was supposed to be managed with medication. Our family didn't have health insurance when I was growing up so I didn't get the meds. As an adult, I had health insurance on my jobs, I didn't take the medication. I don't know why but I do know that I was miraculously healed from that particular ailment. Again, by the grace of Almighty God, a woman I didn't particularly care for prayed specifically for me. I was led by the Holy Spirit to go to her home. Can I just say that He's been there all of the time? At every juncture, He was there.

I was healed after a quarter century of suffering and that healing came without any medication! Little by little progress was made but only as I submitted and obeyed.

WHAT I REALLY WANTED WAS...

What I Really Wanted Was…

I've shared incidents and a few specifics from my first and last relationships that involved domestic abuse and violence. Honestly, all I really wanted was a healthy relationship with a man who loved me and cared for me. I wanted to stay at home, live in a decent house, have a few babies with him and live happily ever after.

I didn't **want** to be promiscuous. I didn't **want** to live in fear. I didn't **want** to be a poor example for my children. But the fact remains that I was all of those things and more. Up until now, I've made reference to God the Father, Jesus who is God the Son, and God the Holy Spirit because they are where all power and teaching came from. I really wanted you to see and to know where I came from and how good God has been to me.

It is typical that we cast blame for the error of our ways on other people. I tried that for years but it doesn't fly. It's easy to attempt avoiding our responsibilities and say that if it wasn't for so-in-so, or if they had done their job I never would have done this or I would have been able to do that. Don't get me wrong; just as I dropped the ball in my parenting role, I am solely responsible for that. However, when it comes to the decisions my kids made, especially as adults, that's on them. Ezekiel 18:20 "The soul that sinneth, it shall die. The son shall not bear the iniquity of the father, neither shall the father bear the iniquity of the son: the righteousness of the righteous shall be upon him, and the wickedness of the wicked shall be upon him." And lastly, Romans 6:23 "For the wages of sin is death; but the gift of God is eternal life through Jesus Christ our Lord."

God does not find pleasure in exacting punishment on any of us but He has an established order, established principles and laws that work when we obey. By the same token, He gives us choices and free will in this life. If we do it His way, we will be rewarded with the gifts He so wants us to have. If we choose to go against His order and principles, the payment will be devastation and death. Sometimes that death will come in stages or bits and pieces, but always bringing pain. Does God forgive? Sure He does. When we ask, He forgives but that does not reverse the principles of His Word. God can extend more mercy but whatever He does is by grace. Did I deserve the treatment I received from my abusers? No. Does anyone **deserve** abuse? Absolutely not. Yet, when I violated my vow to God (rejected Him) and walked into unsanctioned and even forbidden relationships, ***I turned to death*** and ***turned away from the gifts (the life)*** of God. Walking away was my choice. I returned to God but the consequences had been set in motion. Rigor mortis is sure to follow.

In the same vein I don't have an answer for when bad things happen to innocent people. I don't know the 'why' of those things but I do know the 'why' of my transgressions and some of their consequences. Yet, I have still enjoyed and been a beneficiary of the grace of God because I know I didn't deserve His mercy. He just gave it.

Psalm 84:11 For the Lord God is a sun and shield: The Lord will give grace and glory: No good thing will He withhold from those that walk uprightly. KJV

BUT, WILL HE DO THAT... *FOR ME?*

But, Will He Do That For Me?

There is nothing good that God wouldn't do for His children and being one of them is a privilege I will never again take for granted. When I think about the utterly unselfish sacrifice that He made in allowing Jesus, His Son, to pay the price for our sin, I'm humbled. I find God to be the perfect example of the Perfect Father and yet He allowed suffering because there was and is a greater good. There is a much bigger picture and He knew the suffering would be temporary and would afford us reconciliation and salvation. I knew that. I think I took it lightly for years. I knew (or at least I had heard) that God loved me but I still craved the approval, affirmation, and acceptance of the male humans I came into contact with. My lack of appreciation for God's love, His ability, and His unmerited favor for me almost cost me my life. There were times I would compare myself to other women and I'd see their abilities or beauty but found myself coming up short every time. I'd hear their testimonies of how God had brought them out of horrible situations, delivered them, and elevated them. I had no problem believing that God did all of those things…for them. My problem was believing He would do anything ***for me.*** After the back sliding, it was even worse and that's why I had to dive into the Word the way I did. I needed to build up my faith and confidence not in God's ability to deliver me, but in the fact that He ***WOULD*** *deliver me*. I somehow felt 'less than' on all fronts. Comparison isn't a good thing when it's against one another. The only way to compare is to use the Word. That's it!

Luke 1:37 "For with God nothing shall be impossible. Genesis 18:14 "Is anything too hard for the Lord? At the time appointed I will return unto thee, according to the time of life, and Sarah shall have a son. "Lamentations 3:22-23 "It is of the Lord's mercies that we are not consumed, because his compassions fail not. They are new every morning: great is thy faithfulness."

God's love for me (and you) is no less and no more than it is for anyone else. His ability to save and deliver us to the utmost is not stymied or diminished because of our past. I had to get rid of those old thought patterns and replace them with the Truth. I don't pretend to have all of the answers, but I do cling to Hebrews 5:8-14. This helps me in that I was a selfish, immature Christian before I walked away from God. I didn't appreciate or cherish my salvation. After I suffered for a while, I came back with a resolve and a commitment to Him for life. I tasted what He had delivered me from and what He wanted to offer me as His Daughter. He still wants to cover and provide for His children.

Psalm 18:1 I will love thee, O LORD, my strength. **2** The LORD is my rock, and my fortress, and my deliverer; my God, my strength, in whom I will trust; my buckler, and the horn of my salvation, and my high tower. **3** I will call upon the LORD, who is worthy to be praised: so shall I be saved from mine enemies. **4** The sorrows of death compassed me, and the floods of ungodly men made me afraid. **5** The sorrows of hell compassed me about: the snares of death prevented me. **6** In my distress I called upon the LORD, and cried unto my God:

FEAR

&

STIFFLING

&

LACK

Fear & Stifling & Lack

As a child, I heard a saying from adults that went something like this: 'God takes care of babies and fools.' Well, hearing them say that, I simply assumed that they knew what they were talking about. I never seriously questioned it, to be honest with you. Or maybe I should say I didn't question it while I navigated the early years of childhood. Surely, as adults, they were the experts in these matters.

During that time, especially in my culture, children were taught to be seen and not heard. In addition to that, I'd been trained to "stay out of grown folks business – especially their conversations". My understanding and translation of it was to keep my opinions to myself, never let an adult hear what I thought about 'deep' things, and to be careful of which kid I shared my ideas with.

Although I'm a staunch supporter of and advocate for children being respectful, there's a difference between respect and stifling. To put fear in a child to the point of them not feeling safe in speaking their minds, telling the truth, or sharing any important information is dangerous on so many levels.

Respect means maintaining an honorable attitude and tone. That still affords them the freedom to share thoughts, ideas, and facts with others, especially those in charge or in authority. It leaves the door open or future conversations at any given time in a safe environment. Risk may be involved but the conversation isn't avoided because there is mutual respect.

Fear is different. It brings about stifled thoughts, unshared concerns, and an atmosphere of hesitancy. It stops healthy communication, or promotes unhealthy conversations in an effort to avoid confrontation, a beat down, or some other degrading act. This fear is never healthy and honesty or trust never enters the mix. The child knows there's no safety and holds on to that mentality. Avoiding anything risky or unpleasant is held as a priority at all costs. Fear is the foundation and motivation while peace is actually the desired destination.

When children grow up with fear as their basic motivation, not only are they llving under constant intimidation but emotional blackmail. Predators seek these children out to become their victims. It's as if the predator smells the fear and uses it to their advantage. These children don't know their value or worth. They believe they're to blame for every awful and unholy thing that takes place, especially to them. If anything bad happens is their fault, then surely they can't tell anyone what's going on. Predators know this and reinforce it to keep the child quiet and available. The damage only deepens as the years go by and the number of offences and offenders continue to grow. The child, the teenager, and eventually the adult is trapped. They become accustomed to the maltreatment and come to accept it as their normal.

Some become hardened. This, I believe, is an attempt to protect themselves from further hurt, more damage, and more of that ever revolving door that introduces and inflicts pain.

I've had conversations with women who were in brilliant careers, lived in beautiful homes, were pretty as a picture, and had degrees as high as PhD status. Yet, these women carried the same scars as some of my friends who didn't make it out of grade school, were homeless, and wouldn't be considered beauty queens.

All of this was much to my surprise because I'd previously considered them to have it made, have it all together, or even privileged. Real life experience has taught me to never judge or prejudge a book by its cover or a person by their appearance, their title, or any exterior thing.

Certain jobs and ministries have afforded me the opportunity of seeing things up close and personal. Across the board, from women in the highest echelon to those who are not, I've found they actually had similar backgrounds of lack. That lack was foundational and happened early on.

That lack is most often:

1. Lack of a father's protective presence
2. Lack of a father's positive input
3. Lack of a father's involvement in their lives
4. Lack of a father's loving provision
5. Lack of a father's unconditional acceptance
6. Lack of a father's healthy affirmation
7. Lack of a father's emotional support
8. Lack of a father's appropriate physical touch
9. Lack of a father's encouraging words of comfort and correction

TIME TRAVEL

Time Travel

The abuse started long before I had a say in the matter. My confusion and distress began when I was a child.

Have you ever heard of 'Time travel'? I've seen a few movies about it. I've even lost myself in the thought process a few times.

If I could go back and still have the information, insight, discernment and wisdom that I have right now, I would do it. If I could re-raise my kids with the experience and all that I know, I would do it in a heartbeat. Yes, we would make peanut butter sandwiches and go to the beach! If I could go back and care for my mother better and spend more time with her, it would be done in a millisecond.

If I could go back and change the choices I made in selecting mates (and so many other things), it would be a done deal. But time travel isn't an option.

If I could go back and make decisions based on my current insight and information, no brainer. I would go back and choose Jesus earlier, without hesitation. I would stick with Him like glue and behave like a pit bulldog with lockjaw. I would never isolate or distance myself. I would honor Him.

But guess what? I can't do that. Neither can you. None of us can. We're only able to go forward and hopefully ***learn*** from the past. Sometimes, there are no do-overs. Even sharing the experience and wisdom we've gained with others isn't always an option. Not everyone wants to hear it. Nevertheless, I'm determined to do what I can, when I can, as often and effectively for as long as I can.

'If I could' doesn't have to dictate sadness. It can be a learning moment and/or teaching opportunity. It can become proof that we are able to learn from even those negative, painful, and unredeemable moments. If we so choose…

Living in dense, heavy regret and the darker shadows of the past has a way of coloring and shaping our future. Is that how we really want to live? Regretting the past and dreading the future? Not me. At least, not any more.

"Joy is the settled assurance that God is in control of all the details of my life, the quiet confidence that ultimately everything is going to be all right, and the determined choice to praise God in all things". {Kay Warren, in Choose Joy Because Happiness Isn't Enough.}

Philippians 3:13-14 (Amplified) Brothers and sisters, I do not consider that I have made it my own yet; but one thing I do: forgetting what lies behind and reaching forward to what lies ahead, I press on toward the goal to win the {heavenly} prize of the upward call of God in Christ Jesus.

Both my husbands and I enjoy science fiction movies. We watch them separately and together because we both like the many concepts and possibilities they introduce. The thing is that if either of us could take advantage of what SciFi offers in terms of time travel, we would do it.

Now, the only condition would be that we could keep the memory of what wisdom and experience we've accumulated over the years. On the other hand, is the problem that so much of what we're already familiar with and blessed with would have to change. Honestly, without the wisdom God has given us over time, I have no earthly (or otherwise) desire to operate or travel in time to my past or my future. It would simply be a collossal mess and I know it. Besides, what we have in terms of our loved ones and life as we've live it, I wouldn't want to take a chance on losing any of it or them.

Our current lives would be totally different. Our relationship, our careers, our children, grandchildren, great grands, etc., - all of that would be affected and changed. So, although we enjoy toying with the possible ways thngs could have been, wisdom teaches us to be both content and thankful.

Philippians 4:11 Not that I speak in respect of want: for I have learned, in whatsoever state I am, therewith to be content. **12** *I know both how to be abased, and I know how to abound: everywhere and in all things I am instructed both to be full and to be hungry, both to abound and to suffer need.* **13** *I can do all things through Christ which strengtheneth me.*

HE WAS JUST A TOOL

He Was Just A Tool

I've been a writer for most of my life. I just didn't know or recognize it as a gift. I was pouring over some things I wrote back in 1989 and it was so revealing about where my focus had been. Still a prayer warrior and a Believer in Jesus Christ but I was so confused. Every day was a struggle. My state of mind was a mess at the time. Yet, my entry of just a few years later, 1996, reveals a true 180 degree turn from where I was back then.

My life had totally changed from being a controlled, conflicted, confused, and abused woman under the stronghold of fear and defeat. I was becoming a woman of faith with an unbelievably beautiful future of victory in Jesus. Jeremiah 29:13 "You will seek Me and find Me when you search for Me with all your heart." Berean Study Bible Also Acts 17:24-28; Luke 11:9; Matthew 7:7; Proverbs 8:17; Deuteronomy 4:29

It didn't happen overnight. It wasn't an automatic or sure fire thing that came at the flip of a switch. It came with me first realizing the damage I had caused and was, in fact, still causing because I refused to own up to my responsibilities as a Child of God, a mother, and valued human being. I was created to worship God and not my circumstances or other people. After recognizing my true position and my responsibility, I found myself experiencing Godly sorrow and I repented. I didn't know how God would get me to the place I needed to be but that was the beginning. You see, it wasn't really even about my abuser. I experienced an all-out effort on God's part to get a message over to me that I had repeatedly rejected. A lot like the Children of Israel did. Remember their cycle of sin? So do I.

I had toyed with my salvation for years. I took God's mercy for granted because I was always rescued. Always delivered and provided for. Quite honestly, there were times that I knew the outcome of following my emotions would come to no good. I'd done it too many times before. How could I not see where this foolishness was headed? That's always a sure fire recipe for disaster, heartbreak, and unpleasant consequences.

The last man who laid a hand on me had literally become a tool that drew me back to God. Only this time with a vengeance, passion, and a commitment unparalleled by anything else I'd ever experienced. There was no hesitation in my resolve to walk the way God had designed and instructed me to live. I was focused and my heart was changed. I was no longer led by my emotions. Painful as it was at times, I made some of the most difficult choices I'd ever made in my life. **I chose** the Word of God and the path of righteousness over what I was 'feeling'. I chose life. I haven't been the same since. I did something that I didn't know I could. I disregarded my emotions for the sake of doing the right thing. How about you? Are you ready, yet?

20/20 VISION IS CALLED HINDSIGHT

20/20 Vision is Called Hindsight

It's easy to take a look backwards into the past and see what was done wrong. Anyone can do that. The hard part is taking the time to read and study the Word of God and digesting what He says about the future for those who disobey.

Some people disobey because they think they have time to make course corrections. Others disobey because they feel it's time they went after their own happiness. Especially when it seems God is slow in answering their prayer requests for a spouse, a home, a car, a career, or even babies. There's a multitude of reasons including those who just don't believe the consequences of disobedience will happen to them.

Let me just share this with you: There may be many reasons but according to the Word of God, there will not be a single excuse good enough to allow escape from the consequences of our rebellion and sin. Not one!

I remember thinking my abuser was trying to kill me and I was out of fellowship with God. I felt the physical pain of his kicking, punching, and throwing me against walls, but all of that was secondary compared to the loneliness and isolation in the darkness of **life without God**. There's no way to even describe the horror of not feeling His Presence with me. In addition to that was the knowledge that I caused it. I was the one who walked away and this was the result of my rebellion and disobedience. Ezekiel 18:20; Psalm 32; Isaiah 25:8; Revelation 7:17; Revelation 21:4; Isaiah 54:17; Psalm 24:3-6; Hebrews 2:3-18; Mark 8:38.

When I submitted myself, my whole life, my very being, even my plans – thoughts, words, and actions – I began to see things totally different. Don't get me wrong, I'm still learning but there's an atmosphere of obedience in my heart. I don't always get it right. I'll never stop trying and that, my friend, is the difference. I'll never give up again. I'll never allow the enemy to tell me that I'm 'less than' or that I can't make it. If that were true then Jesus died in vain! In fact, John 3:16-18 tells a whole other story and I trust His Truth.

John 3:16 For God so loved the world, that he gave his only begotten Son,
that whosoever believeth in him should not perish, but have everlasting
life.17 For God sent not his Son into the world to condemn the world; but that
the world through him might be saved. 18 He that believeth on him is not
condemned: but he that believeth not is condemned already, because he
hath not believed in the name of the only begotten Son of God.

Please don't wait until every kind of wickedness and tragedy takes place before you give God everything. He can handle it. I'm a living witness. He can. He wants to. He will.

IT'S THE MIND(SET) THAT HAS TO CHANGE

It's The Mind(set) That Has To Change

At some point, it occurred to me that I had been fighting and battling against a tremendous and continuous barrage of negative mindsets. There was so much stuff stored in my mind for years and I wasn't even sure where it came from. Then, I made a decision to follow God fully and He led me to the Waters of His Word. I began to understand why I was susceptible to predators and unholy climates. Over time, after careful and intentional study, fellowship, and prayer, it became obvious that Satan had set me up for complete ruin. The plan was not to destroy just me, but to take down my offspring and anyone he could in my bloodline. He plotted and preyed every step of the way with smoke screens, lies, deception, and everything he had at his disposal to draw me away from God. If he'd been successful in that strategy, my family would be not just in jeopardy but in total chaos. There would be no peace, no true success, no cohesiveness, no love, and no genuine family unity.

This had to stop. Change started with me. I decided against what my emotions dictated. I believed this family could have healthy marriages, healthy familial relationships, clean hearts and minds, holy lives, and right relationships with God. I knew it wouldn't be easy but I also knew that God's Word brings hope to the hopeless, strength to the weak, and light to the darkness.

2nd Corinthians 2:5For though we walk in the flesh, we do not war after the flesh: 4(For
the weapons of our warfare *are* not carnal, but mighty through God to the pulling down
of strong holds;) 5Casting down imaginations, and every high thing that exalteth itself
against the knowledge of God, and bringing into captivity every thought to the
obedience of Christ; 6And having in a readiness to revenge all disobedience, when
your obedience is fulfilled. **Romans 12:1-2** 1I beseech you therefore, brethren, by the
mercies of God, that ye present your bodies a living sacrifice, holy, acceptable unto
God, ***which is*** your reasonable service. 2And be not conformed to this world: but be ye
transformed by the renewing of your mind, that ye may prove what *is* that good, and
acceptable, and perfect, will of God.

I began to diligently work on myself because I understood that the change had to start in my mind. I presented myself to Jesus, holding nothing back. He began a work in me that, at times, left me completely in awe and sometimes completely exhausted.

There were literally moments of what felt like labor pains, days with tears of joy, and nights of severe turmoil. I experienced loneliness, homelessness, misunderstandings, unemployment, lack of transportation, rejection, and pretty much anything you could expect with starting over. But it was worth it. There was a battle going on and I was determined to win because I understood that it was no longer just about me. I knew it was crucial for me to stick with it and get conquer what had held me captive for so long. I don't pretend to be an angel and certainly not perfect. However, I am a Child of the Most High God and we win!

HE LOVES ME TOO MUCH TO LEAVE ME LIKE THIS

He Loves Me Too Much To Leave Me Like This

According to Scripture, when I was adopted into the Body of Christ, I became a new creation. The thing that so many of us miss is that a brand new spirit doesn't translate immediately to a new mind or body. I was still capable of doing the exact same things I had done before salvation. The difference was that I now had the power, the capability and the desire to do life differently. I had the HELP and the HELPER as I was under NEW MANAGEMENT! What a glorious revelation. Did I stumble? Yes. Did I blow it sometimes? Yes. Did I get back up? You bet! The change was in my heart of hearts by the Lord of Lords by His Spirit. I was new but there was specific, detailed, and intentional work to be done in me and on me.

2nd Corinthians 5: 17 ***Therefore if any man be in Christ, he is a new creature: old things***
are passed away; behold, all things are become new. 18 *And all things are of God, who*
hath reconciled us to himself by Jesus Christ, and hath given to us the ministry of
reconciliation;

I still recognized the 'bad boy' types. Yet, I found myself no longer drawn to them, their spiel, or anything they had to offer. I was perfectly content to live the rest of my life without having a man in my life as a companion. It wasn't that I hated them or disliked them. My priorities had changed**. I didn't NEED** a man to complete, affirm, accept, or make me whole! The Person I needed was now the most Central Figure in my life and His Name is Jesus. I didn't have to chase Him down. He was waiting for me to spend time with Him. He valued me. He gave me love and attention. I knew without a doubt that He cherished me. He knew everything about me and still loved me unconditionally. He knew me inside out with all of my flaws and still chose to love me.

KJV Psalm 139: 1 O lord, thou hast searched me, and known me. 2 Thou
knowest my downsitting and mine uprising, thou understandest my thought
afar off. 3 Thou compassest my path and my lying down, and art
acquainted with all my ways. 4 For there is not a word in my tongue, but, lo,
O LORD, thou knowest it altogether. 5 Thou hast beset me behind and
before, and laid thine hand upon me. 6 Such knowledge is too wonderful
for me; it is high, I cannot attain unto it. 7 Whither shall I go from thy spirit? or
whither shall I flee from thy presence? 8 If I ascend up into heaven, thou art
there: if I make my bed in hell, behold thou art there. 9 If I take the wings of
the morning, and dwell in the uttermost parts of the sea;
10 Even there shall thy hand lead me, and thy right hand shall hold me. 11 If I
say, Surely the darkness shall cover me; even the night shall be light about
me. 12 Yea, the darkness hideth not from thee; but the night shineth as the
day: the darkness and the light are both alike to thee. 13 For thou hast

possessed my reins: thou hast covered me in my mother's womb. 14 I will
praise thee; for I am fearfully and wonderfully made: marvellous are thy
works; and that my soul knoweth right well. 15 My substance was not hid
from thee, when I was made in secret, and curiously wrought in the lowest
parts of the earth. 16 Thine eyes did see my substance, yet being imperfect;
and in thy book all my members were written, which in continuance were
fashioned, when as yet there was none of them. 17 How precious also are
thy thoughts unto me, O God! how great is the sum of them! 18 If I should
count them, they are more in number than the sand: when I awake, I am
still with thee. 19 Surely thou wilt slay the wicked, O God: depart from me
therefore, ye bloody men. 20 For they speak against thee wickedly, and
thine enemies take thy name in vain. 21 Do not I hate them, O LORD, that
hate thee? and am not I grieved with those that rise up against thee? 22 I
hate them with perfect hatred: I count them mine enemies. 23 Search me, O
God, and know my heart: try me, and know my thoughts: 24 And see if there
be any wicked way in me, and lead me in the way everlasting.

The other side of that was the fact that He loved me too much to leave me as I was. He knew that the new creation needed some work. The transformation would take time. He was patient. He trained me by His Spirit and His Word. Sometimes it was easy and not difficult to accept. Other times, not so much. He dug deep, peeled away layers of misinformation, guilt, harmful thoughts, exposed painful egregious things done to me, and even words that had been spoken over me and to me. There were times when I felt as if I was sailing on clouds and then times where I felt like I was in the quicksand of past emotions. He taught me how to face those unpleasant thoughts and even the actions of the people I should have been able to trust. Those betrayals along with the ones I committed against myself and those I loved. It has been a long road but I've been fully loved, supported and accepted every step of the way.

WHY STAY?

Why Stay?

Why allow the abuse? Why stay in an unhealthy degrading relationship? I'm sure there are many reasons. I haven't cornered the market on all of them, but I do know of a few that I'll share. ***We're broken.***

Some children aren't prepared for life. They're either sheltered or neglected to the point of being dangerously naïve. Any responsible parent who loves their child would never do that on purpose but it does happen and the child becomes vulnerable due to not being allowed to say 'no' to adults. They really don't know when to say 'no' to anyone. Not being familiar with God and His plan or principles, they don't know that there are times they should say 'no'. They are overly compliant and therefore a delicacy and a morsel of delight for the enemy. They don't know how to navigate through the puzzles and traps that satan sets for them. In defense of the overprotective parent, for the most part they're attempting to protect and train their child. Then that child self-medicates because the pain is so great. No one ever sat them down and explained some of the things they might face in this life so they're not ready.

Neglect can be what family history brings as a repeated action or lifestyle. Say we're dealing with someone who was not permitted to be a child or who was denied basic training and the protection all children deserve. Then that person has a child. What are the odds that this child will receive the kind of training, love, and protection they should receive?

I'm not saying it's impossible, but unless the parent is extraordinary and determined to **NOT REPEAT** that same pattern, we've produced another victim of horrific family history. I do know a few people who have beaten the odds, Thank God! They broke the pattern and cut loose from the chains.

Living in this broken world among broken people is tough. Without God and His training, the chances of thriving and true survival? Nil! Our point of reference, our vantage point, and our understanding of the world around us make up the reasoning power we have at our disposal.

If the bank of information is faulty, then we will make choices and decisions based on that. The foundation is shaky. The walls are thin and the furnishings are cheap. That proves to be nothing less than a recipe for a disastrous life and mountains of regret. *Deuteronomy 6:7 "And you shall teach them diligently to your children and speak of them when you sit in your house and when you walk along the road, when you lie down and when you get up."*

DUE DILIGENCE

Due Diligence

The plot for destroying lives doesn't begin when we become adults. Satan is on his game and working toward our destruction even when we're children. That, my friends, is the reason parents need to wake up and do their due diligence in parenting.

How many of you looked at this picture and went "Awww?" Yeah, I know. Simply adorable. Right? You couldn't conceive of anyone mistreating this little jewel and you certainly wouldn't harm it yourself. I have a nick name, Libby. Some know me well enough and call me by that name.

When I finally left my abuser for the very last time, I was still in contact with one of the neighbors. About 6 months after I left and it was evident that I was done with the back and forth abusive lifestyle, she got in touch with me to give me some news. It seems my abuser and his son had obtained a female puppy. Guess what they named her? You got it. They named her Libby. My neighbor said they had treated the dog so badly that she was compelled to report it. I believe she also said the dog didn't make it. How sad is that?

John 10:10 "*The thief comes not, but for to steal, and to kill, and to destroy: I am come that they might have life, and that they might have it more abundantly.*"

Each of those words? To me they indicate or spell out violence. Thief. Steal. Kill. Destroy. Nothing attractive about either of them if you're healthy or even acquainted with healthy.

It took me a long time to realize it, but what he did to that dog is what he ultimately wanted to do to me. ***BUT GOD!!!*** People, I'm telling you that to resist God is like walking out into a thunderstorm without rain gear, holding an iron rod, and sitting down next to a den of snakes near an alligator farm. Except God delivers you, death is imminent and there is no way out. I stayed because I was broken, misinformed, afraid, unprepared, and walking flat footed in rebellion. I accepted loads of guilt that God wanted to take away from me. I was blinded and led by my emotions. My information was flawed and faulty. I felt really bad about the puppy's fate but understood that it could very well have been me. Clearly, he was a sick man. Why couldn't I see that before I walked into that situation? Again, my emotions led me right into the trap of satan and the arms of a dangerous man. Yes, I knew some scripture. Yes, I knew my actions were wrong. Problem? I was in my feelings and had no power to resist him on my own. I ended up trapped because I submitted to emotions and not to God.

James 4:7 "Therefore *subject yourselves to God. But resist the devil, and he will flee from you." (also translated as *submit*)

Subject or submit to God.

Resist the devil.

All voluntary but if done, the result is a slam dunk for us instead of a runaway enemy! Worth every tough thing we face. Obedience to Christ takes the Strength of the Holy Spirit. As we are doing the subjecting and submitting to Christ and resisting the devil, we have to rely on Something and Someone stronger and wiser than we are naturally. My emotions and/or feelings won't come under submission unless I take control and give them to the Lord for his power to be instituted and applied. That's when I win.

SIMPLY COMPLICATED

Simply Complicated

Dr. James Dobson has a book out called "Emotions, Can You Trust Them?" He explores and explains a lot and some of it is so simple! I consider it a classic and it has been revised at least once.

Simple yet complicated when we're not properly prepared to handle the sin factor. Some things are principles and they don't change. For instance, take the law of gravity. It doesn't matter if one is a Christian or a non-believer. To take a step off of a 16 story building will most likely result in the same consequences for both. SPLAT! I know. Gross and graphic perhaps but still true.

Following and trusting our emotions can be deadly. Most of us experience a myriad of emotions throughout any given day. From elation to anger; confusion to clarity; peace to conflict; happiness to hate and on it goes. *Ephesians 4:14 "...so that no longer we might be infants, being tossed by waves and being carried about by every wind of teaching in the cunning, in the craftiness of men with a view to the scheming of deceit." (See all of Ephesians 4:11-15)*

It isn't that God expects us to be like robots and behave as if we don't have emotions. That isn't the point. What He offers is Help to sort out those emotions and Strength to move beyond them when they're not fit or right for the occasion. *John 15:26 When the Helper comes, whom I will send to you from the Father, the Spirit of truth who goes forth from the Father, He will bear witness concerning Me.*

The Spirit of Truth. We need Him so that we have the ability to distinguish between what is right and holy and proper. After that, the strength to do what we should do is paramount. All of that is found in The Holy Spirit. We need to be able to see and follow Jesus. That won't happen without Him. Our feeble attempts are just that in light of what the enemy of our souls can do. Alone and vulnerable is where we are when we try doing anything without Christ. We're found drowning and overwhelmed without The Rock of Ages. We're tossed to and fro, back and forth, up and down when we leave Him out of our everyday decision making. I used to try and please or impress people. No matter what I did, someone was always displeased or unimpressed. It became crystal clear to me that I was in the wrong frame of mind. My purpose, my mission, and my passion for and in this life are to please an Audience of One. That One is God. The Trinity – Father, Son, and Holy Spirit. Doing that brings a peace which flows like a river. I mentioned Dr. Dobson's book and I recommend it no matter what age or stage of life we're in.

Joyce Meyer also had a series years ago called "Love Is". I checked to see if it was still available but it wasn't. I'm sure there is comparable material that will teach you how to recognize true love but you'll have to search it out. These are just a couple of the people God used to help me on my journey to health. I can't say back to health because I never knew it until my walk with Christ became serious.

HOW DID I ESCAPE?

How Did I Escape?

So, how did I get out of the pattern of abuse? What was it that gave me the courage to acknowledge, repent, receive the grace, walk in God's Strength, and escape the impending doom that hovered over my life every single day? *Revelation 12:11 And they overcame him by the blood of the Lamb, and by the word of their testimony; and they loved not their lives unto the death. Luke 21:31-32 Simon, Simon, Satan has askea to sift each of you like wheat. 32But I have prayed for you, Simon, that your faith will not fail. And when you have turned back, strengthen your brothers."...*

The True and Living God of Glory began to speak to me in ways I still don't fully understand but I knew it was Him. It finally hit me that this situation was about more than just me. I either had to buckle down and grow up or sacrifice all I held dear. My thinking began to change and process with such clarity that it was almost like a movie in 3-D.

That very strong and mighty steel-like hold that had influenced and warped my mind for years was suddenly gone. I saw my responsibility as a mother above the temporary pleasures of this world. I accepted ownership for my sin, errors, and mistakes. Then I repented. Not just an 'I am sorry I got caught' kind of admission but the kind that says, 'Lord, I'm ready for a 180 degree turn. I'm ready for a new lifestyle and I want to do whatever I can to help my children overcome this mess I've created for them.' I finally saw them as the precious gifts that God had given and entrusted to me. I was humbled beyond measure.

When He spoke to me, I was completely convinced and encouraged that He was more than enough. Had I been duped before? Yes. Had things happened to me that were unfair and out of line? Yes. Was He able to make it all up to me AND my babies? YES! Was I afraid to step out? Sometimes, I was but I knew that I had a testimony and my life was in God's hands if I dared obey Him. I also knew that others would be able to benefit from where God had brought me from and was bringing me to.

Was it hard at times? Yes indeed but He never left my side. *1 Thessalonians 3:3 "But the Lord is faithful, and He will strengthen you and guard you from the evil one." Jude 24 "Now to Him who is able to keep you from stumbling and to present you unblemished in His glorious presence, with great joy—"*The Lord took me through the steps of recovery. Honestly, I had symptoms of what felt like PTSD/shell shock for a bit but I clung to God and His Word for life.

God guided me, as to what, when, and how to do what needed to be done. It was difficult. It involved a number of people, places, jobs, and other resources. He did it in a way that I never would have come up with. He built up my confidence over time in His ability to rescue and provide. He taught me that ***not only was He enough but I was enough***. I didn't need a man to complete me. All I needed was Him (Holy Spirit) to finish what He had started. I freely admit that He is still working on me and that I am a work in process. Yet, He has been faithful and then some.

Honestly, I don't know if I had ever thought of myself as 'enough'. But GOD said it and I was being trained. I was in training for becoming a trainer. It was one thing to get out but what was God wanting me to do once I got out? Realizing He doesn't waste anything was major in that training because He began to reveal purpose. It was beautiful.

YOU'RE NOT ALONE IN THAT BOAT

You're Not Alone In That Boat

As anyone who has been in therapy will tell you, whether it is physical or mental, there is usually pain involved to move forward in the healing process. Facing the part we may have played in the injury or damage is tough.

Sometimes in physical therapy it's almost like reinjuring the part that was broken. Inflicting more pain to what's already hurting just doesn't make sense, at least not to the natural mind. I've found God's therapy for healing and recovery to be that way at times. The tears I've cried and the pain I've faced? I can't describe what it has been like but I can tell you that it was worth it to find myself on the right side of healthy and whole.

1Peter 2:24 "He himself bore our sins" in his body on the cross ... ... who his own self bare our sins in his body upon the tree, that we, having died unto sins, might live unto righteousness; by whose stripes ye were healed.'

I don't think anything can prepare a mother for the kind of predicaments children get themselves into. My mother passed away a number of years ago but I still remember the look on her face when she realized the state I was in. Whether it is physical abuse, mental abuse, financial abuse, emotional abuse or whatever, we take the people we love into those hives of hell with us. They may not be there literally but they're there in our agony. They cry for us. They pray for us. They labor and sometimes have sleepless nights because of us. So, while I only considered myself and eventually my children, there were other people in the boat with me.

Then there's the kind of injury where you didn't do anything to deserve it. These are the things others do to us: Divorce, abortion/murder, adultery, fornication, rape, molestation, abuse, neglect. All of these things hurt us but they do untold damage to others as well.

A friend of mine once told me that her divorce was bad but it wasn't just the act itself that hurt. It was the fact that there was no funeral. At least when someone dies you can begin to get closure because you won't see them anymore. Then, in time, healing begins. In a divorce, there's a good chance you'll see the person and be constantly reminded of the hurt, the break, and the pain. It may take longer to heal.

With abuse, neglect, rape and molestation you experience similar emotions. After the offender dies, even if you've confronted them about their crimes against you, the pain remains because they don't apologize or repent. It's kind of like a wound that's constantly open and exposed to the elements. That's when the forgiveness becomes a release for the victim. Release it through forgiveness and release yourself to healing. Some offenders will deny it and/or ignore you. Some will even attempt to turn the offence around to point blame in your direction. Mine did that. It became my fault. Some will try to convince you that it's all in your mind. It never happened. It's all in your mind…it's your imagination. In other words, you're crazy!

Some of my pain was that way. Men who had betrayed my trust were still alive and going on with their lives. It was as if I didn't matter and what they did was nothing. I don't mean just as an adult. I mean the men who hurt me as a child and kept living their lives while I tried to understand why they … the trusted male members of our family and community… would do something like that. There was an unspoken code of keeping quiet that didn't help matters any. ***This is why, WOMEN, you need to protect your children. Choose who and what you expose them to! In today's vernacular, STAY WOKE, please.***

As with any process, healing takes time. To get from point A to point B, sometimes seems impossible. The bridge seems long and endless but to put it in God's hands is always the best way to do it. *Hebrews 10: 29How much more severely do you think one deserves to be punished who has trampled on the Son of God, profaned the blood of the covenant that sanctified him, and insulted the Spirit of grace? 30For we know Him who said, "Vengeance is Mine; I will repay," and again, "The Lord will judge His people." 31It is a fearful thing to fall into the hands of the living God....*

I would love to tell you that I crossed every 'T' and dotted every 'I' along the way. I'd love to tell you that I didn't make a single mistake in word or in deed or even in attitude.

That just wouldn't be true. Initially, I wanted my offenders to suffer and I wanted to witness it as it happened! I wanted them to experience pain as I had. I wanted them to die a very slow and agonizing death. Then God came through again. He reminded me that I needed an attitude adjustment and a reality check. It can be so easy to condemn people to hell because of our pain and opinions. Capable of pity parties and judgmental attitudes that outrank almost anything, I needed correction and a reality check. True to form, God provided both.

When it comes what happens to us in childhood, we don't have control over those things. As Christians, we are commanded to forgive and move on. As adults, that same principle exists, forgive and move on. That means forgiving the people who did us wrong and forgiving ourselves for being in a position of sin and exposing others to the undeserved consequences.

Colossians 3: 12 Therefore, as the elect of God, holy and beloved, put on hearts of compassion, kindness, humility, gentleness, ano patience, 13bearing with each other and forgiving each other. If anyone should have a complaint against another, even as also the Lord has forgiven you, so also you. 1 Corinthians 6:11 And that is what some of you were. But you were washed, you were sanctified, you were justified, in the name of the Lord Jesus Christ and by the Spirit of our God.

Please don't misunderstand this. **God is NOT saying to ignore offences and sin.** Not by a longshot. When a crime has been committed, especially against children, it needs to be reported and then handled by law enforcement. What He is saying though, is that we, as His Children, are held to a Standard that is above the world's standards. We can forgive and still handle business. We don't hold grudges or make up and exact our own brand of retribution. We can hate the sin but still care about the sinner. That's what He did for us and we were on our way to hell when He did it!

I especially want you to notice that even though we are forgiven, there are still consequences for sin. Some of us tend to forget that little tidbit and hold people in prison (in our hearts and churches) even when God lets them out. We hold them yet we want God to continually forgive, set us free, and sometimes even overlook our offenses. Not so. God is just…for real.

Paul, my husband recently preached a couple of sermons that resonated with me as a very important part of the healing process. As children of God, we are created to worship. We can worship ourselves, our pain, our past, or any number of things but worshiping God is essential. One point he made was that we may be in a state of waiting. Waiting is something most of us don't like to do. What should we do while we wait? We should worship God while we wait. We would find peace and a particular joy if we choose to worship while we wait on the Lord to reveal or rework things in our lives.

Another important point he made was to those who are wounded. Should we carry around that invisible placard or billboard that tells the world we're suffering? Should we carry that sign around in an attempt to solicit pity and 'understanding' for the wrongs done to us? Should we ignore and 'stuff' our feelings and become martyrs in our woundedness? The answer highlighted WORSHIP again. We should worship while we're wounded.

To find the proper way to do that doesn't mean a prescribed method as we wait even in our woundedness. It looks different for each of us. The main thing, I believe, is to be open to what the Lord would say and how He would lead us. Personally, I found it to look different depending on where I was in my journey and how much time I was spending with Christ. Anywhere from lifting my hands, singing songs, crying ugly tears, laughing at myself, exercising or whatever was needed to take care of my health, listening to praise music, sharing my victories and my fails, thanking God out loud, memorizing scripture, studying scripture, lending a shoulder for someone else to cry on, volunteering, looking at the stars, appreciating what and who I have, on and on but always recognizing that He was right there with me…and He still is.

PAID IN FULL

Paid In Full

In His correction, the Lord reminded me that He is a Gentleman and He only accepts willing participants as His followers. He doesn't put a gun to our heads and He's never forced me to do anything I didn't want to do. Now, that being said, He does have a way of revealing our motives and the condition of our hearts to us. The flip side to that is He reveals His purity, love, affirmation, acceptance and His heart to us.

I've had some very close calls with death. I've had some wonderful and most glorious times with God. There are people who wish me evil and God calls me to love them. His Word tells me that if there is to be a reckoning in addition to the civil authorities, He is the one to handle it, Not ME. Sometimes that's a hard pill to swallow but I know He's always right. He has proven to me over and over again that it is my choice whether I obey or disobey, whether I follow Him or not. He doesn't highjack my mind or decisions. He simply provides me with His instructions along with the power and ability to follow.

He has been merciful in that the consequences could have been so much worse. Yet, in His grace and great love, I didn't get what I really deserved.

Romans 6:23 For the wages of sin is death, but the gift of God is eternal life in Christ Jesus our Lord. John 3:16 For God so loved the world that He gave His only Begotten Son, that whosoever believes in Him should not perish but have everlasting life.

God still pays the required wages of death for our sin. For those who would accept Christ as Savior, Jesus has paid the price and has taken our place. He received what we should have gotten.

It remains the same for anyone who would accept Christ as Savior. In my judgmental mode, I was picking and choosing who should be forgiven and who should not. The thing I overlooked was the sacrifice of Jesus Christ Who was the Only One worthy and willing to handle that office.

My abuser(s) really did me a favor in that they turned my eyes toward Jesus. There was nowhere else to go for a true healing. There were other things I could have done. Other things I could have tried but I had tried enough. I had reached my limit and it was Him or nothing. I chose Jesus. *Joshua 24:15 But if it is unpleasing in your sight to serve the LORD, choose for yourselves this day whom you will serve, whether the gods your fathers served beyond the Euphrates, or the gods of the Amorites in whose land you are living. As for me and my house, we will serve the LORD!"*

I had given the enemy enough of my time, my talents, my family and my energy. The wise choice was the God who really loves me. I was made to worship Christ. I finally 'got it' and the rewards have been great. A bed of roses? You might say that because real roses come with thorns. I'm okay with that since crushed roses have a lasting aroma.

Struggling with the hard choice of doing what you know is right to do as opposed to following your unreliable emotions? Let's keep it real.

It has been over three decades since I had to deal with any kind of abuse in my home. Yet, I still remember what those emotions led me to and how difficult it was to walk away. In fact, I still have that occasional reminder in the form of a terrible recurring nightmare. It happens less frequently but still at least once or twice a year. That nightmare is a reminder of just how far God has brought me and how He delivered me from the hand and plans of the enemy.

It took a long time for me to recognize the futility of it all. Suicide attempts, loss of income and property, reputation ruined, damage to my children, and unnecessary worry for the people who genuinely loved me. All of that grief came in addition to putting another stain on the church at large. Somehow you may still feel that chasing a man, waiting for him to come around and get it right is worth it. After all, he's the father to your child or children. Besides, you love him and he says he loves you and the kids.

Well, let's go this route. Is he the kind of man you want your daughter or granddaughter to end up with? Is he the kind of man you want your son to become? If there is anything in you that says "no", then I suggest you step back and take a look at your life with him. Lady, you are teaching by example whether you mean to or not. They are learning from you…good, bad, or indifferent. They're picking it up and one day your choices will influence and color their choices. Perhaps you say that they're too young right now to pick up anything. Really? When was the last time they did or said something they 'caught' from you? Or him? The early years for kids are called the formative years because their minds, opinions, and true personalities are being decided and formed. They are like little sponges soaking up whatever is around them. *Proverbs 22:6 Train up a child in the way he should go, and when he is old he will not depart from it.*

Is this written in stone? Is it something that is sure fire and without a doubt going to happen? Will your daughter choose the kind of man you have chosen? Will your son become the kind of man you've chosen? Will you absolutely be risking and exposing your future grandchildren to the misery of this lifestyle? There are no guarantees. Just as there is no guarantee that if you do everything right, your kids are going to choose wisely. Bottom line is, they will have free will and choose what they want just like you did. Your part is to give them the best possible optics you can. Make sure they're taught correctly because if you don't then that's on you. The heartache can be minimized. The guilt factor can be lessened. The regrets don't have to be as huge as they will be if you don't try and get it right. Give them the material, the tools to at least know what is right and normal.

I can tell you right now that if you don't, you'll be opting for the kind of pain I wouldn't wish on my worst enemy.

Please don't get me wrong. I am not telling you to go against scripture. I am, however telling you to study scripture. Get some counseling from a certified Christian counselor. By all means, please, approach and petition God for your answers.

CONFORMED
OR
TRANSFORMED

Conformed or Transformed?

Diversion and distraction. These are effective tools the enemy uses to pull us away from God's mission in our lives. The ultimate goal is to be useful and actively on the path that the Lord has laid out for us. If my attention shifts away from the goal, there is a good chance that I'll miss the mark. We have to remember to renew our minds because the enemy is exceptionally good in tactical maneuvers. He has studied us over the years. No, he doesn't know our future but he does know our history, our past. He uses that information to his advantage. Deceit. Diversions. Lies. Accusations. Doubt. He will bring up an old fact, a previous action or behavior to trap and keep us locked in the prisons of regret and guilt. If we're stuck in the past, it is doubtful that we will move forward to accomplish future successes.

When our view is obscured by preconceived notions and current conditions, the difficulty is in how we gain clear vision.

Matthew 14:25-27

The disciples thought they were seeing a ghost but they were actually seeing Jesus in action. It was a lesson in Jesus' school of reality. Things that first appear to be terrible and awful could turn out to be a miracle in the making.

Our thoughts lead to our belief system and actions. Whatever we're going through is something we think about either positively or negatively. It is rare that we have random neutral thoughts. Our minds have been trained since before birth. We are made in the image of God.

Genesis 1:26

God is a triune being and so are we. We are body, soul, and spirit. God is Father, Son, and Holy Spirit. Retraining is necessary because we have been trained to think and behave a certain way all of our lives. Now, as Children of God, the Word tells us *Romans 12:* [2](AMPL) *And do not be conformed to this world [any longer with its superficial values and customs], but be transformed and progressively changed [as you mature spiritually] by the renewing of your mind [focusing on godly values and ethical attitudes], so that you may prove [for yourselves] what the will of God is, that which is good and acceptable and perfect [in His plan and purpose for you].*

Whatever the end result of our experience turns out to be, we must be mindful that the adventure begins with a thought. We must guard our minds and renewal begins with the Word of God. That retraining has to be from the pure and unadulterated Word. *Psalm 119:10 With my whole heart have I*
sought thee: O let me not wander from thy commandments. 11 Thy word have I hid in
mine heart, that I might not sin against thee. 12 Blessed art thou, O LORD: teach me
thy statutes. 13 With my lips have I declared all the judgments of thy mouth. 14 I have
rejoiced in the way of thy testimonies, as much as in all riches. 15 I will meditate in thy
precepts, and have respect unto thy ways. 16 I will delight myself in thy statutes: I will not
forget thy word. 17 Deal bountifully with thy servant, that I may live, and keep thy word.
18 Open thou mine eyes, that I may behold wondrous things out of thy law.

LAYING THE PAST TO REST AND MOVING ON

Laying The Past To Rest and Moving On

I was going through some old pictures and reminiscing the other day. It seems as though time is moving faster for me these days. I'm pretty sure it isn't but it feels that way. Single word descriptions come to mind. I'm reminded of where I was when all of the drama took place. Then I asked myself this question: I know what I was feeling but what was I thinking?

Making a conscious decision to walk away from the Living Lord of Glory was complete insanity. Yet, He hasn't wasted a single thing I walked into. So much of my life experience has been told either in print or in person. He doesn't have a problem with exposing the ugly side of where I was because that's exactly where so many women are right now. There was a time that I thought or at least behaved as if no one else had issues, at least not compared to mine. That whole mindset has changed. I no longer find myself automatically resisting God as if it's a reflex action. My desire today is to stop the foolishness and cooperate with God. I identify and empathize with the plight of so many people and the road they're traveling. We say, in Christendom, that "It's Not About Me." We've learned well how to speak 'Christianese' and rely on our former Christian acts. But bottom line, God is present and accounted for in the here and now. We should be, too.

Philippians 3:12Not that I have already obtained all this, or have already been made perfect, but I press on to take hold of that for which Christ Jesus took hold of me. 13Brothers, I do not consider myself yet to have laid hold of it. But one thing I do: Forgetting what is behind and straining toward what is ahead, 14I press on toward the goal to win the prize of God's heavenly calling in Christ Jesus. 15All of us who are mature should embrace this point of view. And if you think differently about some issue, God will reveal this to you as well. 16Nevertheless, we must live up to what we have already attained.

I don't 'make' things happen but living in the past can arrest our progress in the Kingdom of God. Are we attempting to sustain ourselves and others today off of the acts and fruit from yesteryear? God can and He does take the past, repackages and repurposes it. That's His prerogative.

However, there comes a time **we** are required to go on and grow up. It is time for us to move and walk into our purpose with intentionality and thank God for our past.

1 Corinthians 13:11 When I was a child, I talked like a child; I thought like a child, I reasoned like a child. When I became a man, I set aside childish ways.

My foolish acts of the early days should not hold me captive for today's agenda. Former successes and accomplishments shouldn't be my only contributions or points of reference. If I allow that to happen, I'm not only cheating those who need to believe failure isn't final. I'm saying the wins from the past are enough and I can 'retire' from the faith, so to speak. We are constantly presented with opportunities for growth. Those will become testimonies either for or against the Kingdom of God. Not works based for the sake of works, but cooperation with God for the building up of the Body of Christ.

Like it or not, we're all in this thing together. We may have different types of baggage but the desired destination is the same. We begin this journey as helpless infants. We receive various types of information; have different resources, parents, and gifting. Even our opportunities differ. But at the end of the day, we will come to the unswerving and unavoidable time to meet the Lord to receive rewards or punishment. I sincerely want us to realize that partial obedience is still disobedience. Can we really afford that?

Hebrews 9: 27Just as man is appointed to die once, and after that to face judgment, 28so also Christ was offered once to bear the sins of many; and He will appear a second time, not to bear sin, but to bring salvation to those who eagerly await Him....

I have been guilty of playing church. I have made vows and promises. Some I kept and some I didn't. We are without excuse, Friends, it is high time we realize who the real enemy is because there is a war going on and I am determined to remain on the winning side.

2nd Corinthians 10:3 For walking in flesh, we do not wage war according to flesh. 4For the weapons of our warfare are not fleshly, but divinely powerful toward the demolition of strongholds,5overthrowing arguments, and every high thing lifting itself up against the knowledge of God, and taking captive every thought into the obedience of Christ, 6and having readiness within to avenge all disobedience, when your obedience may have been fulfilled..

I don't know when or how I'll be leaving this earthly realm or this earthly body. What I do know is that if my thinking is right and I'm right with God, there is a home waiting that Jesus makes available to me. You have that same opportunity. No matter what your role is or has been in this life, God loves you.

I was once really good at blaming other people or my circumstances for my flaws, my sins, and my current condition. Yes, there were adults who could have done a better job of looking after my well-being. Honestly, I could have done a better job, as well. Even the most conscientious among us probably could have done some things differently and better. But I have come to the conclusion that whatever has happened has happened. We might as well take the broken down trees damaged by the storms and begin to rebuild, make some fires, and provide shelter for current and coming generations. I may not be able to go back to fix the past but I don't want to live in it, either. I can take what God has given me and use it in today's world for good.

My sisters and brothers in Christ are not my enemies. Atheists, agnostics, and abusers are not my enemies. Politicians, police, lawyers, protesters and aliens are not my enemies and I'd be foolish to spend my energy fighting with them. That's how we lose ground and lose focus on the main thing.

Nehemiah 6 speaks of the distractions 2 *That Sanballat and Geshem sent unto me, saying, Come, let us meet together in some one of the villages in the plain of Ono. But they thought to do me mischief.* 3 *And I sent messengers unto them, saying, I am doing a great work, so that I cannot come down: why should the work cease, whilst I leave it, and come down to you?* 4 *Yet they sent unto me four times after this sort; and I answered them after the same manner.*

God's Word explains what it is that we're fighting against. This is a spiritual war and the enemy is banking on us not paying attention. He draws us in by distraction and deception. We become distracted and don't see the bigger picture as to what's really happening. We spend time blaming, complaining, finger pointing, reminiscing and wallowing in self-pity while he ravages our homes and families.

There is a remedy but we have to be willing to follow God's instructions, be discerning and allow the wisdom God gives us to operate in our lives. That's when we get things done that are important to God. When we know what the Main Thing is and focus on it, I believe we'll be more effective as a Body of Believers. When we stop jockeying for positions, power, prestige, and press time, we'll see the changes necessary to turn the tides of justice and morality because we will have recognized that God is the Main Thing.

Our comfort and fleshly satisfactions are not the main thing! Well, when am I going to be happy? When will I get to enjoy life? When? When? When? When?

I would venture to say that the when actually depends on us. When we acknowledge God and His Agenda, His purpose for our lives, and repent of our sin and participation in the blatant sin of others, I think we just might realize that joy and happiness are found in Him. Our contentment is only found in Christ. Our desperate attempts to ignore and disallow Him are the things that cause us to be unhappy and discontent. The void we try to fill with other things and people will not work. There is no substitution for Christ. Nothing and no one will ever be enough to replace Him…Ever.

SUBMITTED TO JESUS AND EACH OTHER

Submitted To Jesus and To Each Other

September 18th, 1991 marked the beginning of our lives together as husband and wife. At the finishing of this book, 2020 – I've enjoyed 29 years of marriage with my husband, Paul. Imagine that. He and I have been married ***to each other.*** I highlight that because we've both been married to other people. If you had known either of us in the very early years of our marriage, you'd realize what a miracle 29 years is. The one thing we honestly had in common and had going for us was our genuine love for Jesus Christ.

We had so many things that were against us in the beginning. It was touch and go. I was constantly on an emotional roller coaster. We had opposition from pretty much all sides. We come from completely different backgrounds. We are a 'blended' family. There is a considerable age difference. I came with baggage that I recognized and admitted as well as some I wasn't aware of. He came with baggage that he didn't consider baggage and a mindset of superiority. Now, put all of that together and mix it with other people, their drama and expectations, adult and teenaged children, inexperience at total honesty in love, stubborn attitudes, financial reversals, health challenges, as well as varying degrees of relational hurts and losses. Not to mention our own expectations of each other and the disappointment that comes with that. We went to counseling, both lay and professional.

We were seriously on the verge of breakup at least once or twice a year. Then something happened. About 6 or 7 years in, Paul (my husband) told me that as far as he was concerned, ***divorce was not an option***. How is it that two broken and damaged people, plagued by the past and burdened by current events, made it in marriage for 29 years still loving and respecting one another?

*Ephesians 5:21 Submit to one another out of reverence for Christ. 22 **Wives, submit to your husbands as to the Lord.** 23 For the husband is the head of the wife as Christ is the head of the church, His body, of which He is the Savior....*

I'm about a lot of things but I do not play with God's Word when I understand it. I attribute his statement to me an epiphany he received from the Lord and passed it on to me. I'm pretty sure we wouldn't have made it if he had not come to that conclusion. The above scripture reveals the heart of God for married couples. I see it as a call to honor, respect, and prefer the other unselfishly over themselves.

Although, that was and is the noble and right thing to do, can you imagine how difficult it was for me to fully trust him after the relationships I had been in? I know it wasn't an easy thing for him, either. I struggled to try and get it right for years. I questioned his love for me, obsessed over his mistakes, his lack of knowledge, and his inexperience even. Today, I love him more than I would ever have imagined possible. He has proven time and time again just how much he loves and treasures me and our relationship. But you know what? None of this would have been possible had we not SUBMITTED first to God and then to each other. Our success as a couple and individually, and I don't mean materially or financially, depended on trusting God. We've been able to benefit and bless the Body of Christ in the area of real relationships because of our struggles. We do not walk in fear. We walk by faith. God does that with broken things (and people) submitted to Him.

I fully recognize something else that was and still is paramount to our staying together and loving each other. He had fallen in love with Jesus and loved Him more than he loved anything or anyone, including me. He couldn't have loved me properly if he didn't love Christ more. Christ by the Holy Spirit actually taught him how to love me.

The same goes for me. I had to love Jesus more than I loved anything or anyone else, including Paul. The Lord took me to school and I'm still in school. I'm attending class to make sure I get it as close to right as I can in my human form.

Hopefully, the following pages will be useful and help you to find ways of evaluating and navigating your way to a fuller life in the Word of God. Abba Father, Our Precious, Holy, Righteous, Mighty, All Powerful, All Knowing, Ever Present God will take care of you.

PULL OVER, LET'S TALK ABOUT THAT

PULL OVER, LET'S TALK ABOUT THAT

Reasoning for Reflection and Refining

Isaiah 1:18 "Come now, and let us reason together,"
Says the LORD,
"Though your sins are like scarlet,
They shall be as white as snow;
Though they are red like crimson,
They shall be as wool.
19 If you are willing and obedient,
you shall eat the good of the land;
20 But if you refuse and rebel,
you shall be devoured by the sword";
for the mouth of the LORD has spoken.

Reason: talk over, talk through, discuss

Reflect (ion): think, consider, ponder, think about

Refining (refine): sharpen up, improve, hone

He's Faithful Even When I'm Not

Jeremiah 29:11-14 [11] For I know the thoughts that I think toward you, saith the LORD, thoughts of peace, and not of evil, to give you an expected end. [12] Then shall ye call upon me, and ye shall go and pray unto me, and I will hearken unto you. [13] And ye shall seek me, and find me, when ye shall search for me with all your heart. [14] And I will be found of you, saith the LORD: and I will turn away your captivity, and I will gather you from all the nations, and from all the places whither I have driven you, saith the LORD; and I will bring you again into the place whence I caused you to be carried away captive.

I've begged, bargained and at times, even tried to bully my way into blessings. I insisted on having my own way. I wanted the results of obedience but not the act or the process. I certainly didn't like the instructions required in obedience to the Word of God. The simple truth is that God has a way we don't always agree with so we try to make adjustments to fit our desires. We try to compromise with something that isn't designed to be changed or adjusted. It comes with an unwavering 'AS IS' clause and if we follow it, we'll reap the benefits. If we don't, then expect fallout.

The Word of God shines the light on the fact that my desires are not always best. Sometimes, that's because I'm so emotionally charged that I can't see past those feelings. I don't always think of the benefits of the process, of waiting, or of the lessons learned while waiting. I am usually thinking about the pain involved.

Jeremiah 29:11-14 teaches a profound lesson. In this book and previous passages, God's people had been disobedient and rebellious. Not unlike us, they found themselves in a pickle, an unhappy place. The Lord was reassuring them that He would deliver them but they would have to wait awhile. In other words, He does hear when we call or ask for relief but we have to wait for His timing. He sees us right where we are.

As was their plight, I've been in some messy situations. Faced with the consequences, I wanted out of them immediately. Though I tend to be impatient and even headstrong at times, God reassures me that He wants to lead me into a bright and prosperous future. Though I may have caused this situation and may still be headed in the wrong direction, He's always looking out for me and He is never confused. Even having caused the mess that I'm in, He's working to bring me to my best end with a prosperous future and a hope of better days to come. The deal is that He isn't emotionally distraught or distracted. He has a plan. He's working His plan. He has my best interest included in that plan and my best option is to do it His way going forward.

Pull Over. Let's talk about that.

Lamentations 3:22-23 It is of the Lord's mercies that we are not consumed, because His compassions fail not. They are new every morning: Great is Thy faithfulness.

Faithful: loyal, constant, and steadfast;

Have you ever experienced a time where you let your emotions get the best of you?

Describe what was going on at the time

Did you ask God to change the circumstances?

Did you beg or bargain to try and get God to comply?

Bottom line, what happened and how did it turn out?

How was your attitude throughout the whole process? How were you emotionally?

Do you see it differently now? Does it still sting when you think about it? Can you see any progress in your level of maturity because of it? Are you glad it wasn't an affirmative answer to your prayers?

Just Do It!

Proverbs 22:6 "*Train up a child in the way he should go: and when he is old, he will not depart from it.*"

Train (TheBusinessDictionary): to coach, prepare or grow in a direct manner with a clear and achievable outcome. Train or coach another person to acquire more skills or improve existing ones.

There's a tendency amongst some parents, church folk, and people in general to tell children (and younger Christians) to "just do it!" or "because I said so".

In the mind of the person making the demand, this sounds simple and quite reasonable. To the person receiving the demand, it could prove to be an overwhelming challenge. The recipient needs to know exactly what "it" is. If no training has taken place, "it" could mean many things. The chance of satisfying an unknown expectation is slim to none. The level of frustration is increased because no clear set of instructions or directions have been given. Training for me is best when I get to see it and then perform it over and over again. Taking notes reinforces what I'm told and what I get to do. Hearing it, seeing it, writing it down, and then the hands on experience makes it real and memorable for me.

That's what this verse is bringing to the forefront. People need training. If they're not trained, why expect them to do anything the right way?

Train up a child in <u>*the way he should*</u> go - Hebrew "Initiate the child at the opening (the mouth) of his path." When he comes to the opening of the way of life, being able to walk alone, and to choose; stop at this entrance, and begin a series of instructions, how he is to conduct himself in every step he takes. Show him the duties, the dangers, and the blessings of the path; give him directions how to perform the duties, how to escape the dangers, and how to secure the blessings, which all lie before him. Fix these on his mind by daily inculcation, till their impression is become indelible; then lead him to practice by slow and almost imperceptible degrees, till each indelible impression becomes a strongly radicated habit. Beg incessantly the blessing of God on all this teaching and discipline; and then you have obeyed the injunction of the wisest of men. Nor is there any likelihood that such impressions shall ever be effaced, or that such habits shall ever be destroyed. Clarke's Commentary

One of my major complaints in the corporate workplace was the lack of good training. One job in particular had a person who had been there over 20 years. Nothing was written down and everything was in her head. Training was "watch what I do a couple of times, listen to me for a couple more times, then go do it". Can you imagine the level of vexation that could cause?

Whether it be children in the physical sense or children as in Babes in Christ, let's take the time to properly train the people we mentor. It's of major importance.

Pull Over. Let's talk about that.

What is the best training experience you've had? And who trained you?

What is the worst training experience you've had? Who was responsible for it?

Have you ever trained anyone? Were you patient? Were you kind? Were you thorough?

Is there a particular area that you need to be trained in as a Christian?

Do you know of anyone who would do a good job in training you? Who? Why them?

What is your favorite style of learning? Observing? Hands On? Reading the instructions?

If you had the opportunity, what would you say to the person who didn't do such a good job in training you (whatever the subject was)?

Are you aware and do you appreciate the fact that everyone doesn't learn the exact same way? Can you respect that fact?

Approval Addiction

Ephesians 4:11 So Christ himself gave the apostles, the prophets, the evangelists, the pastors and teachers, [12] to equip his people for works of service, so that the body of Christ may be built up [13] until we all reach unity in the faith and in the knowledge of the Son of God and become mature, attaining to the whole measure of the fullness of Christ.[14] Then we will no longer be infants tossed back and forth by the waves, and blown here and there by every wind of teaching and by the cunning and craftiness of people in their deceitful scheming.

One of the problems we face is that we (some of us) want ***everyone*** to like us. Well, that's not at all realistic. We're anemic as a whole because we're not whole as individuals. Our expectations don't line up with the Word of God and that means we try to get the approval of people who are just as flawed as we are (except some of them don't know it or won't admit it).

We have all of the approval we need from Christ but we try to get more from people because we haven't accepted Him as **ENOUGH**! I don't mean we should go out and behave as if other people don't exist, or that they don't matter. I'm saying that God will equip us if we'll stand still long enough to be trained. Some of us church hop as if it's a game and that translates to confusion and instability. Then, there's another group who come to church regularly but have no intention of following what God says we're to do. God has people in place to teach us but we have to stay where He directs to get proper training. Why? When we receive the Truth, we are then able to walk in and pass that Truth on to others. When we mature, then we can help others mature as well.

The Word of God is not something everyone will like. If we live and proclaim His Word, that in itself will tick somebody off and they'll take offense. In other words, they're not going to like us because of 'What' and 'Who' we represent.

We have to get over this approval addiction. If we don't, we'll remain weak and ineffective in and for the Body of Christ. We can't afford to be affected or influenced by who does or does not like us.

Take note of the fact that most of the people who lauded and applauded Jesus soon became His haters. They didn't like a lot of things about Him and the outcome was that He was crucified. Yet, He remained consistent in proclaiming what was right. He was not swayed by popular opinion or political polls. He went with what His Father said. That will often cause some people to be uncomfortable. They'll be offended. They won't like you. They won't approve of you. Will you still do what Our Father says? Will you stand or will you fold due to an Approval Addiction?

Pull Over. Let's talk about that.

How important is it to you for other people to like you?

Has it always been that way for you, even as a child?

Are there people you want to like you more than others?

Do you sometimes find yourself not saying important things because you're afraid it will alienate you or ostracize you from the person you need to say it to?

Would you say this is a type of self-imposed bondage? Is there more than one person you feel that way about?

II Timothy 1:7 For God has not given us the spirit of fear but of power, love, and a sound mind.

What does this scripture mean to you in light of what is being discussed here? Does it apply to you at all?

How might you grow from fear to faith in this area? What does it mean to 'do it scared?

Breaking Your Heart to Save Your Life

Psalms 71:20-21 *You who have made me see many troubles and calamities will revive me again; from the depths of the earth you will bring me up again. You will increase my greatness and comfort me again.* John 16:22 *So also you have sorrow now, but I will see you again, your hearts will rejoice, and no one will take your joy from you.*

Emotionally, I've not always been stable. Shocking, right? I still have some residue and left over baggage to deal with. I used to pray out of my emotions a lot. Something I wanted to take place or cease was the norm of my focus in prayer. Most of those prayers were totally *NOT what God wanted*, yet it was *what I wanted*. So I prayed (out of my emotions) hoping He would say 'Yes'.

This is one thing I've learned as a parent, you shouldn't always say "Yes" to your children's pleas. If you love them, there are some things you must say "No" to. As a parent, you know some things that your children don't. Good parents don't say 'yes' to a toddler's demands of crossing the street alone. Why? The parent is aware of the dangers of oncoming traffic, the toddler's inability to navigate steadily, and the combination of all other aspects in crossing a street. They say 'no' to teenagers who want to stay out until the wee hours of the morning. Why? The parent is aware of the temptations available at all times, the teen's inexperience with life, and the combined dangers that present themselves in unsupervised situations. Somebody said: "ain't nothing open after midnight but legs." I could go on but I believe you get the picture.

I've learned this concept and the reason behind it, but I'm way past dealing with my children as little kids. They're all grown and I see the results of some of my decisions.

When I asked God for some of the things I wanted, it seemed reasonable and even fair to me. Yet, many days and years later, I am so thankful that He gave me the right answer. Sometimes the answer was a flat out 'NO' and I found myself heartbroken at the time. Other times He said 'Wait'. That didn't go over so well, either. I've been guilty of ignoring His 'Wait' and His 'No' and leaving a trail of tears behind me. Then there were the times where He said 'Yes'. My appreciation of Him grew with each answer because I know He always has the best outcome in mind.

He has broken my heart many times. He intentionally allowed the pain of disobedience to teach me why it's important to accept His answers. My broken heart mended. My life was saved because He always knew the reason for every answer even when I did not. I fell headlong into traps the enemy had set. This happened when I wouldn't accept what God was saying to me. God was faithful and waited patiently for me to quit flailing and fighting so that He could save me. I'm reminded of Jonah in the belly of the fish. All he had to do was obey and accept what God was saying for him to do. It wasn't until he found himself trapped in that stinking, murky and uncomfortable place (where disobedience will ultimately take all of us), that he realized how ridiculous it was to fight against God! So it is with me and perhaps you, as well. I've learned to look to, obey, and trust God because He knows the full story, from beginning to end.

Pull Over. Let's talk about that.

Seriously, has God ever told you *to do something* **OR** *not to do* something and you rebelled?

What were the consequences of your actions? Were other people involved/affected?

Would you call the consequences 'trouble'? Do you think you deserved it?

If you had opportunity to have a 'do over', what would you do differently?

Psalm 119:71 It is good for me that I have been afflicted; that I might learn thy statutes.

In light of the current discussion, can you see any redeeming value to Psalm 119:71?

Is this something that you can appreciate or apply in practical terms for your life? If yes, how? If no, is there a better scripture to describe what you learned if anything?

Do you believe emotions can be good or bad? What's your take on making emotional decisions?

Can You Hear Me Now?

Sometimes my hearing aids work almost perfectly and I can hear really well. At other times, the noise of other things crowd out what's being said. I clean them, change the filter, switch batteries, or go to a quiet place for optimum clarity of sound. Other days, I discover repairs or overhaul is needed. That's what some of us need for our spiritual hearing. Cleaned by the Word, change what we let into our lives and hearts, recharge and recommit to Christ, get alone with Him leaving the noise of the crowd (the politically correct and culturally accepted). Perhaps we wouldn't be so confused if we got completely new ears.

Revelation 3: 19 As many as I love, I rebuke and chasten: be zealous therefore, and repent. 20 ***Behold, I stand at the door, and knock: if any man hear my voice, and open the door, I will come in to him, and will sup with him, and he with me.*** *21 To him that overcometh will I grant to sit with me in my throne, even as I also overcame, and am set down with my Father in his throne. 22 He that hath an ear, let him hear what the Spirit saith unto the churches.*

Maybe, just maybe, we've allowed debris from certain conversations to become a problem in how we hear God. Maybe it's leftover trash someone dumped into our minds. Maybe it's an attitude of entitlement. Or yet again, it could be unforgiveness or anger that's become a root of bitterness we won't let go of. It could be unconfessed sin, habits, addictions or some other thing that God wants to deal with. Problem is that we hold it too precious to release to Him. That becomes a 'hearing' problem (I may hear but don't want to obey). The soul is the seat of our decision making. We are bombarded with things that this world pours into our lives. These come and plant themselves in our minds; they sit waiting for us to say it's okay to gain entry. Once they gain entry, they gain control. Our spirit is there as well, patiently waiting with the counsel of the Word of God as guidance. The soul is the command post. It is the Board of Directors where decisions are made to go either right or left, straight ahead or backwards, stand still or to roll over. The information is available. The choice is ours to make one way or the other. The exact consequence or outcome may not be known but there is enough information to decide. Our flawed training has been to go with how we 'feel' or what we 'think' and against the Word of God. If immediate pleasure and/or bodily gratification is more important to us, we err on the side of sin. When the scales are tipped on the side of a wrong decision, we will pay the cost along with others we take with us. I don't know it all but I do know this: When I allow my emotions and affinities to lead me instead of what I know is right to do, not only is my hearing impaired, but I'm heading for disaster. That's when I need a washing, a cleansing, and a renovation of the heart. I need to hear clearly when there's a conversation going especially when lives are at stake. I can't afford to have the debris cloud my decision making abilities. Neither can you. Disasters can cause my hearing to improve but the cost can be very high.

Pull Over. Let's talk about that.

Does it ever 'feel' like you're getting more 'no' responses from God than 'yes' answers?

Why is it important to ***NOT ALLOW*** your emotions to lead when it's time to make important decisions?

When you're not sure about the decision you need to make, what do you think the best strategy would be until you know for sure?

Do you have anyone you trust and can go to for sound, biblical advice? Do you see the need for such a person in your life? How honest will you allow them to be with you?

When it comes to accountability, are you in relationship with anyone you're accountable to and you're completely honest with? Why or why not?

Would you consider yourself: a loner, a social butterfly, a mix between the two, or something else entirely, depending on the situation?

In retrospect, how many mistakes have you made by depending on your emotions and not enlisting 'wise counsel'?

Growth Opportunities

As a child, I grew up in an agricultural society. We traveled along the East Coast of the U.S. We harvested fruit and vegetables in accordance to the seasons.

There were times when we'd arrive too early to commence harvesting. The crop might not be ready, the weather might be inclement, or the equipment wasn't prepared for our use. Depending on the conditions, we would have to wait until we got the go ahead from the owner. Instead of murmuring and complaining, we found ways to occupy our time until we could actually begin harvesting the crop. We waited for the crop to mature because no one wants immature fruit for consumption.

*Eccl. 3: 1 To everything there is a season, and a time to every purpose under the heaven: 2A
time to be born, and a time to die; a time to plant, and a time to pluck up that which is planted;3A
time to kill, and a time to heal; a time to break down, and a time to build up;4A time to weep, and
a time to laugh; a time to mourn, and a time to dance;5A time to cast away stones, and a time to
gather stones together; a time to embrace, and a time to refrain from embracing;6A time to get,
and a time to lose; a time to keep, and a time to cast away;7A time to rend, and a time to sew; a
time to keep silence, and a time to speak;8A time to love, and a time to hate; a time of war, and a
time of peace.*

That is what I'm reminded of and prompted to consider when hard times, tough times, or inconvenient things are found on my plate. When I'm faced with things outside of my wheelhouse or comfort zone, I'm challenged to either learn from them or prolong the process by complaining. No, it isn't comfortable or pleasurable. It isn't what I want. Yet, the Lord encourages me to explore and experience all of that season. If I get out of it prematurely, the fruit won't be ripe for eating. If I stay in it too long (meaning I still need to trust His plan), the fruit will be useless as well.

So, wherever I find myself, there is an opportunity for growth. As a Child of God, He knows exactly how long that season should last. He knows the conditions required to grow me as a tree with useable fruit. He knows who is going to need the fruit that will be produced from my seasons of growth. He also knows the things I need in order to be ready to allow others to benefit from that fruit.
We all have problems and experience issues that we would prefer not to. Yet, there is a purpose for all of it. I don't believe God wastes anything in our lives. When the time comes, He wants us to be ready for the harvesting, to be useful for others and to have learned to be thankful and flow in whatever season we're in. Sometimes, I need a good cry or I need to forget something, or embrace

someone. Whatever the season, God is available and He wants us to remember that because we're never alone.

Pull Over. Let's talk about that.

Have you ever had to deal with tough things or hard times? Are these things that were not your fault? List a few of them.

What effect did those times have on you? Can you see anything good that came out of the experience?

Have you been able to use those experiences to encourage someone in your walk with Christ? If so, how did you approach the subject of your difficult times?

As you encouraged them, was it awkward to talk about?

Has anyone ever encouraged you during your hard times by telling you about their experience in tough times? Did it help? Was it relevant? Did you appreciate them sharing?

Do you believe there is a purpose for everything we experience even if it isn't something that is fun or pleasant? What is the fruit from a tree used for? Is it for the tree? Can it be used to feed others? Is it useful to the tree at all?

What/Who Do You See in the Mirror?

I Corinthians 13:11 When I was a child, I spake as a child, I understood as a child, I thought as a child: but when I became a man, I put away childish things. 12 For now we see through a glass, darkly; but then face to face: now I know in part; but then shall I know even as also I am known.

In school, on one hand, I was considered smart and caught on quickly. Then, on the other hand I was horrible at detecting traps such as guys who were not good for me. Relationally, I was clueless. Many years and a bunch of bad relationships later, I put a few things together. I surmised it was time to change a few things. I didn't really do that until I faced my past behavior, tried to determine why I behaved that way, and understood the need for change. After all, I was the common denominator in each of those relationships.

As a child, I saw myself as inferior even though many considered me gifted. Somehow, because of the image I had of myself, I didn't see the 'gift' at all. Being book smart didn't make me smart in relationships. Yes, the school work was easy most of the time, even when I missed days of school. Teachers marveled at how I was able to do it. However, when it came to guys and the choices I made, it's a miracle that I'm still alive.

Home life had a lot to do with that. My father was absent, my mom was a single parent doing the best she could to raise three children under not-so-favorable conditions. During that time, race relations, body image, unruly hair and a face I wasn't happy with, big feet, buck teeth, and nothing to color the future with brightness made things a tad difficult. Needless to say, my self-image was lacking and it didn't get better with the passage of time. That same image of 'lack' carried into adulthood. It wasn't until I came face to face with a loving God who cared for and gave Himself for me that I began to experience a sense of worth. I began to take responsibility for my own actions and stopped blaming my parents, my surroundings, and my 'lack' for my bad behavior. I began to see what my choices did to me and my children as well as how those choices could change. I understood that what I saw in the mirror as physical features wasn't at all who I really was and that made all the difference in the world. It took time but I finally saw that my childish vision and version of myself needed to change. My focus and my understanding needed overhaul so that I could function as a contributing adult in this society. I needed a new perspective and God gave me that. It wasn't overnight. In fact, I may have been a slow learner but I finally got it. I wanted different results so I had to make different moves. I began to see clearer. I grew by studying and applying the Word to my life, staying in fellowship with other Believers in Christ, and taking the time to commune with Christ. I'm no longer tossed to and fro nor am I confused about who I am. The God of all creation loves me! I'm not puffed up or proud but I appreciate who God says I am and the investment He made in securing my salvation. It was time for me to grow up and I have. Not perfect but rest assured I'm not the same child wearing dark glasses that I used to be. I thank God for rescuing and teaching me that I have worth right here, right now.

Pull Over. Let's talk about that.

What was your image of 'you' when you were a child?

Was that image a true image or was it something other than the truth?

Looking back, where do you think the image you had of yourself come from?

Were those thoughts reinforced or encouraged by those you honored or respected?

Did anyone ever tell you that the thoughts/images you had should change?

If you could go back and encourage yourself, counsel yourself, what would you say? What do you think would be different if you could change the thoughts and images you had at time?

Do you think it's too late to take your own advice now as an adult?

Sometimes It Just Doesn't Fit

1 Samuel 17:38 Saul clothed David with his armor; he put a bronze helmet on his head and clothed him with a coat of mail. [39] And David girded his sword over his armor. Then he tried to go, but could not, for he was not used to it. And David said to Saul, I cannot go with these, for I am not used to them. And David took them off. [40] Then he took his staff in his hand and chose five smooth stones out of the brook and put them in his shepherd's [lunch] bag [a whole kid's skin slung from his shoulder], in his pouch, and his sling was in his hand, and he drew near the Philistine.

Have you ever started a new job and were told you had some leeway and flexibility as to how you worked the schedule and projects required? Someone did the job before but you weren't locked in as to how it got done because the company was more interested in the results than the process. Of course, there was a training period and transitioning from the way the other person did it to how you saw fit to get it done. Then the trainer had a different point of view on how much freedom to give you in doing the job. So, that complicated matters and created some friction in the mix. Really, all you were trying to do is learn the job but it was cramping your style with all of the requirements and steps the trainer was putting on the process. They didn't mean any harm but it was just way too much for you. Their rules and regulations made you feel as if you were suffocating and performance on the job began to suffer.

After a heart to heart talk with the trainer, they released you to do it your way and it was a slam dunk! Everybody wins and you celebrate because you were no longer encumbered or weighed down with somebody else's 'stuff'. Sometimes, we admire the way other people do things because they seem to get so much accomplished and make it look easy. But what we need to remember is that none of us are exactly alike. We're different. Our make-up varies. Some of us are similar in likes, dislikes, DNA and so on but for the most part, we are not the same. That speaks volumes to me because that means we need to give each other the freedom to operate the way God made us. We shouldn't try to force or hardline prescribe how each person navigates, conquers, or fights their individual battles. My armor may not be what the next person needs. My method may not work as well for someone else. Unless it definitely goes against the Word of God, I don't have the right or authority to pass **my opinions** off as ***the Gospel.*** We all have to find what works for us and that means an individual walk with God. I can give counsel, suggestions, and support but to demand it be done 'my way' would be a mistake and an infringement on their rights. People have a right to choose. God gives that to all of us. If He gives that right then it is a sure thing that I should do the same. What works for one person, suits that person but could be totally wrong and just not a good fit for another. The respect factor must be observed and we'd be wise to keep that in mind, always. Not to ever compromise the Word of God but to know that we should free people up to serve in the capacity God gives them. We need to allow them to find the perfect fit and their place in the path God has laid out for them.

Pull Over. Let's talk about that.

Have you ever seen an outfit of clothing that looked absolutely great on a model or a mannequin? Were you tempted to purchase it or try it on but found it just wasn't you?

What did you do with the clothes after seeing what they looked like on your body? Whatever you did, why did you do it?

Has anyone ever told you that you have a specific style that works for you? Do you believe that you do or are you in search of whatever that is?

Do you ever wonder what it would be like to be another person or personality type? Why or why not? Name one of your 'good' personality traits. Why is it 'good'?

Do you believe God made you to be uniquely who you are or who you are becoming?

What is it like when you're just being yourself?

Has anyone ever tried to shame you for being yourself? What did you do to defend yourself or did you accept it? Have you ever, knowingly or unknowingly done that to someone else? Why or why not?

The Not So Jolly Green Giant

Psalm 42:5 Why, my soul, are you downcast? Why so disturbed within me? Put your hope in God, for I will yet praise him, my Savior and my God. 6 My soul is downcast within me; therefore I will remember you from the land of the Jordan, the heights of Hermon—from Mount Mizar

Some of my favorite vintage television commercials featured a character called The Jolly Green Giant. The giant used a special patented process to be sure his product was at its best. Now, I'm sure that was a great thing for the consumer because the taste was fresh and tasty as well as nutritious. However, if the vegetables had been consulted, I'm guessing they might have resisted that painful 'special process'. If given the choice, even though knowing it might be a good thing in the long run, being made aware of the probable end results doesn't always inspire us to endure the process. It has to be something more.

There are memories, things, people, and times I would much rather avoid because their presence is painful. I don't like it when I'm squeezed and feel as though I'm in a press. The process sometimes seems to be extremely slow and the pain excruciating. So much so that I find it hard to believe anything good will come of it and I just want the pain to stop! Many times the pain ceases or at least lets up for a bit and I can take a breath. Even at that, I'm often pensive and waiting for the next wave because I know the break is temporary.

Most of us don't like to experience pain, not even the slightest needle stick! We like it when things are going well and there are no fires to put out. When the bills are paid, the family is fed, and we're getting along – that's a great feeling but we know that in this world, it doesn't last forever. That, all by itself, can cause us to be sad. Yet, the psalmist asks the question of his soul: Why are you unhappy? The remedy given is to put our hope in God. Praise our Savior and our God. Remember Him and what He has done in times past.

I find it helpful to write down the good, the bad, and the ugly times I experience. It helps me when I need encouragement. When I'm having a rough day or series of days, I can go back and see, remember, and bring back to my mind the times that God came through for me. I'm reminded of times that I couldn't see a way and the future seemed bleak and dim but God made a way. It's during those times that I am persuaded that no matter what, He is always with me. I am never alone. I may not like the situation but I know that God is real. God loves me. God cannot lie. He is always working for my good and His glory. He works on my behalf and His plans are for me to be in good health even as my soul prospers.

What I need to remember is to feed my soul the nutritious Word of God so that it/I will prosper. I may not always be jolly but I can always recognize the goodness of the Lord, even during the process where times may not be so happy. It is ***through*** the process that the valuable and nutritious things are brought out. Those are the things will be good for anyone who needs it – now or later.

Pull Over. Let's talk about that.

Psalm 119:71-73 Amplified "It is good for me that I have been afflicted, that I may learn Your statutes. The law from Your mouth is better to me than thousands of gold and silver pieces. Your hands have made me and established me; Give me understanding and a teachable heart, that I may learn Your commandments. "

What does this scripture mean to you? Do you think it applies to any portion of your life?

Have you ever asked God why certain things were happening to you? Are there things happening to you now that you would prefer not to go through?

Do you believe God will use this part of your life for His glory?

What is the difference in going through a situation and going through it ***well?***

When going through a hard time, do you still trust that God is in control? How do you know if you're 'teachable' or not? How familiar are you with scripture?

When it comes to your emotions, do you obey according to how you feel or according to the principles in God's Word?

Do you learn better by experiencing things yourself or by the experience of others?

Have you ever rejected the counsel of other people because you didn't like the person?____

Nests and Potty Chairs

The saying goes something like this: 'You can't stop birds from flying over your head but ***you can*** stop them from making a nest in your hair.'

Remember that a lot of stuff goes on in nests besides baby birds being fed. That nest is where they have their breakfast, lunch, and dinner but for all practical purposes, it's also their bathroom. Now, I may not know the whole process because I haven't studied the 'private home life of birds'. However, I can't think of any other way the whole system could possibly work if after eating, their bodies didn't allow for elimination. No one wants waste products in their hair, right? So, how about in their heads (their minds)?

*Romans 12:1-2 "Therefore I urge you, brothers, on account of God's mercy, to offer your bodies as living sacrifices, holy and pleasing to God, which is your spiritual service of worship. Do not be conformed to this world, but be transformed by the renewing of your mind. Then you will be able to test and approve what is the good, pleasing, and perfect will of God." **2 Timothy 1:6-7** "For this reason I remind you to fan into flame the gift of God, which is in you through the laying on of my hands. For God has not given us a spirit of timidity, but of power, love, and self-control." **Revelation 12:11** "And they overcame him by the blood of the Lamb, and by the word of their testimony; and they loved not their lives unto the death."*

Years ago, a young woman asked me this question: How do you make it stop? The depression; the pain and anguish of downward spiraling thoughts; the way you think and feel that feeds the depression? At the time, I didn't have an answer for her. Full disclosure is that I was still trying to find the solution for myself. However, over time, I found the answer for stopping the birds from making a nest in my head. Today, it's a whole other ball game and it isn't nearly the struggle it used to be. I've been through the fires of depression, oppression, and all kinds of ungodly impressions. I have learned what works for me to overcome.

I asked God to help me. I took to the scriptures and I immersed myself in them. I played music that would lift my mood and change the atmosphere. I sang songs that included the Word or the principles of the Word. I guarded my mind and the company I kept. I forgave offenses quickly (real or imagined). I made it a point to be thankful for life and what God had already provided.

Following the principles of scriptures gave me the answers I needed to fight off depression. I know this sounds simple but after over 25 years of fighting suicidal tendencies and debilitating thoughts, I found the answers I needed. That's what worked for me and it still does. Each of us has to find our own way but the principles of God remain the same. Seeking Him is the first step, always. Sticking with Him is the goal for a lifetime. It pays off. I have not been perfect in my walk nor have I been perfect in following the solution I discovered. I do know this: it works whenever I do it the way God prescribes. I have faltered. I have slipped and fallen and yet, God has always been faithful to help me get up when I repent and ask for His help and forgiveness. He never fails.

Pull Over. Let's talk about that.

Sometimes, I get off track when my emotions are involved. I mean, I know the right thing to do but then I start to feel used or disrespected and I want to fix the situation out of my hurt or pain and outside of God's way. Has that ever happened to you?

Do you have friends who give you advice from the Word of God? Do you have friends who give you advice that doesn't line up with the Word of God? Who do you listen to most? Does Romans 12:1-2 Ring true for your life?

Do you ever operate from information you gained outside of what you know is right? Something that conflicts with and is opposite to the Word of God?

When/if you do that, how do you make course corrections?

What does the term "junk in, junk out" mean to you?

Exactly how do you stop 'birds from making a nest in <u>your</u> hair/head'? Are there things you believe you should get rid of in your thinking even now? How can you do that? Does it really matter?

What are some good things you've learned over the years? What do you need to be careful about when it comes to information you hear and accumulate? Are you being careful? Why or why not? Are you courageous enough to do what it takes? Even if it means distancing from people you love?

When it's a God Change

"Do not remember the former things, nor consider the things of old. Behold, I will do a new thing, now it shall spring forth; Shall you not know it? I will even make a road in the wilderness and rivers in the desert" (Isaiah 43:18-19 NKJV).

When it's time for change in our lives, there is often a season of preparation, a process necessary to help us let go of that place of comfort or familiarity so that we can embrace what He (God) wants to do next. When God orchestrates change in our lives, it is very seldom easy and often involves pain. Kind of like childbirth, I suppose. No matter how intense the pain during labor, one look at that child makes it all seem worthwhile. Nevertheless, 'God Changes' are beneficial for our growth and maturity. Why does it take difficulty, pain, or dry times to bring about change? Although I have observed other people and peeked into their journeys, I can really only speak from my own. I tend to settle into habits, routines, and comfortable places because they're familiar. I know what to expect, how to handle myself, and how to navigate through or around bumps in the road. When something comes along to either disrupt, make me uncomfortable, or I'm unsure how to deal with an unfamiliar situation, I prefer not dealing with that. I mean, what if I do or say the wrong thing? What if I mess it up? What if I embarrass myself or others? What if it hurts too much? What if my flaws are exposed? What if they're mean to me? What if I'm reprimanded? What if...?

No matter the situation, I've always found God to be faithful, true to His Word and His specific promises to me. I don't like pain but pain is an indicator of an underlying problem. The pain of rejection, being misunderstood, ostracized, lied on, labeled, ignored, used, kicked to the curb, disrespected, etc.? These places can cause me to cling to the familiar because it's safe for the most part. Yet, God calls me to step out of that place of comfort. When His purpose has been accomplished, it's time to move on to the next place He wants to use me. Oh, I've tried to use about as many excuses as anyone else would: Lack of education, age, past mistakes, other's opinions, how someone treated me or my loved ones, how I look or feel. I've got a laundry list of excuses. But guess what? None of them work.

You see, I've discovered something. God has equipped me for a specific path. I am uniquely qualified with a certain skill set to provide sustenance for a select group of people. Some of them will deal with me one on one, some will listen in a congregation, and still others will read what needs to be communicated. My former pain and the way God prompts me to write about it will be used by the Holy Spirit to assist those people in accepting the freedom that Jesus died for. God provides the connection. The gifts and talents that God has deposited in me are tools that He will use to bring them to the foot of the Cross. After all this time, I finally understand my place in the grand scheme of things. I plant, nurture, encourage, and teach. I am a light and a city set upon a hill. I'm vulnerable, transparent, and available. I listen to God and I obey. That's it. God has chosen the skills. He uses me to accomplish His purposes.

How about you? Are you ready to cooperate with the 'God Change'? Let Him use that former pain for His Glory? Will you allow your life experiences to become a catalyst, springboard, or an inroad for someone else's freedom? Will you be the source of nourishment for someone in need? Someone did it for you, right?

Pull Over. Let's talk about that.

Who does God say you are? What does His Word say about you? Do you believe it? ______________________________

____

Does it seem like a burden or an imposition when others want more of your time than you normally give?

____

____

____

____

Have you ever felt desperate to spend time with another person because you believed they had something you needed?

____

Have you ever believed God was directing you to spend time with someone to share your gifting with them? Did you obey the call? Why or why not?

____

____

____

Is change, even if it's for a good cause, difficult for you? Is it harder or easier now than it was when you first received Jesus as Your Savior? What's different?

____

____

Is there anyone you consider your 'Go To' person when you need to hear the truth? Do you have difficulty looking in the Word and seeing yourself or do you normally see other people and their need to change?

____

____

____

Are you honest with yourself and others when there's a chance that your honesty might hurt some feelings?

____

Some of us will avoid conflict at all costs, even at the risk of lying. Is that your testimony?____

If I Could... But I Can't

Have you ever heard of 'Time travel'? I've seen a few movies about it. I've lost myself in the thought process a few times.

If I could go back and still have the information, insight, discernment and wisdom that I have right now, I would do it. If I could re-raise my kids with the experience and all that I know, I would do it in a heartbeat. Yes, we would make peanut butter sandwiches and go to the beach! If I could go back and care for my mother better and spend more time with her, it would be done in a millisecond. If I could go back and change the choices I made in selecting mates, it would be a done deal. If I could go back and make decisions based on my current insight and information, no brainer, I would. If I could go back and choose Jesus earlier, there would be no hesitation. I would stick with Him and behave like a bulldog with lockjaw. I would never distance myself. No questions asked. I would honor His track record.

However, I can't do that. Sure, I would if I could, but I can't. None of us can. We're only able to go forward but we can learn from the past. Sometimes, there just are no do-overs. Even sharing the experience and wisdom we've gained with others isn't always an option. Not everyone wants to hear it. Nevertheless, I'm determined to do what I can, when I can, as often and effectively for as long as I can.

'If I could' doesn't have to dictate sadness. It can be a learning experience and/or teaching moment. It can become proof positive that we're capable of learning from even those negative, painful, and unredeemable moments. If we so choose... Living in dense regret and the darker shadows of the past has a way of coloring and shaping our future. Is that how we really want to live? Reliving and regretting the past and dreading the future? Not me. At least, not any more.

"Joy is the settled assurance that God is in control of all the details of my life, the quiet confidence that ultimately everything is going to be all right, and the determined choice to praise God in all things". {Kay Warren, in Choose Joy Because Happiness Isn't Enough.}

Philippians 3:13-14 (Amplified) Brothers and sisters, I do not consider that I have made it my own yet; but one thing I do: forgetting what lies behind and reaching forward to what lies ahead, I press on toward the goal to win the {heavenly} prize of the upward call of God in Christ Jesus.

Nothing suggests to me that time travel is possible. I've had some Deja vu moments but that still doesn't say I traveled through time. A much loved Pastor of mine often says that the only time we have is right now. I can't go back for a do over and neither can you. What we can do is to pay attention to Psalm 90:12 which speaks to us appreciating and using the time we do have. Using it wisely because there are no guarantees of what the future holds. We should treasure and use it wisely because what we do today has a profound effect on the future.

Not just our individual futures but the future of those we hold near and dear. Remember that.

Pull Over. Let's talk about that.

Do you ever day dream or find yourself doing serious time in 'I wish I had' or 'had not'?

If the opportunity presented itself, what three things from your past you would change?

Why would you change those things? What negative impact have they had?

Since you can't change those things, do you think grieving for what you think is lost would be appropriate? If so, how long should you grieve? What does scripture say?

How would changing those three things change life for other people in your world?

Have you ever talked to God about this area of your life at all? Have you listened to what He has to say about it?

Is guilt a part of what you experience when you think about those three things?

What is the difference between condemnation and conviction? Can you see the importance of operating from the position of power that God has given us? Are you ready to move from condemnation or self-loathing that the enemy tries to burden God's children with?

The Bottom Fell Out

Looking forward to a leisurely walk on the beach, I was in the kitchenette about to wash our breakfast dishes. Nice, hot, soapy water ready to oblige. Then, what seemed in slow motion, I saw dishes tumbling and water splashing to the floor along with glasses, cutlery, and a frying pan. My well prepared dish water was now all over the kitchenette floor, in the carpet and on my feet because... the sink had fallen into the cabinet below. At first I stood in shock and disbelief with dish towel in hand trying to absorb what had just happened *even as it unfolded!* The entire sink had come apart with all its contents emptying at my feet!

Still in celebration/shock mode, the call to the front desk was made. Humor helps but this was surreal. Maintenance came. We repacked, changed rooms, unpacked again, and tried to normalize the rest of our trip. Did I mention Paul's gout had kicked in the day before we left home? Yet, we still enjoyed our time with each other...*Sunrise, broken sink, great big beautiful ocean, gout and all.*

Sometimes, life is like that. When you least expect it, things can quickly and dramatically spin out of control dropping water balloons, acid bombs, or Molotov cocktails on your parade. We choose how we respond and determine how we go forward. Our anniversary fiasco was very mild and even comical when compared to some of the other things we've faced both as a couple and individually. Is that true for you, too?

Life has twists and turns that can be challenging. It might be an illness, a wayward child, a job loss, a financial reversal, an accident, a betrayal, or even the loss of a loved one. Each overwhelming and devastating but there is hope. In the midst of living life, it becomes abundantly clear: We are not in control and tomorrow is not promised.

Our best option is to live today as if it is our last. Follow the dictates and commands of God and enjoy ***this moment*** and ***these people*** to the full. There is a series of books that promote "Don't Sweat the Small Stuff". The concept or general theme is that it's all small stuff so don't over react or stress.

God has given us this very precious gift called life. I haven't always understood or valued the gift. In fact, it has taken me a long time to come to this most important revelation and appreciation. When it comes to regrets, my biggest ones are because I didn't grasp the brevity or the fleeting opportunities to 'carpe diem'.

Ephesians 4:11) "Not that I speak in respect of want: for I have learned, in whatsoever state I am, therewith to be content. 12) I know both how to be abased, and I know how to abound: everywhere and in all things I am instructed both to be full and to be hungry, both to abound and to suffer need. 13) I can do all things through Christ which strengtheneth me."

It is guaranteed that most of us will experience some tough things and times. The secret many of us miss is that even though things will rock our boats, we don't have to allow those things to throw us into the murky waters of depression. I may not know the full of my future but I do know the One Who holds my future and He is in charge.

Pull Over. Let's talk about that.

Can you think of a time where it seemed multiple 'bad' things were happening to you or to people you love?

Do you tend to mull over hard things or wallow in self-pity during hard times?

Is there anyone you talk to about the hard things? Do you speak to God and do you ask Him why these things are happening to you or your loved ones?

Remember the book of Job? Why do you think his friends came to spend time with him as he went through the hard times?

Were his friends truly concerned about what was happening to him? Would you say they were genuine friends? Why or why not?

Have you ever been misunderstood by your friends? Have you ever misunderstood or wrongly accused others?

Have you ever been upset with God? Be completely honest about it. Examine yourself and determine whether this is something that needs to be addressed especially if you feel He has dealt unfairly with you. Study his conversation with Job and let that settle for a bit before you speak.

Can you say there have been times that He could have let things get much worse than they actually did? What does that say to you about God and His mercy?

Must Be Nice

Believe it or not, that statement can mean more than one thing and I think I've experienced a few. Allow me to share one in particular with you.

1 Corinthians 13:4 "Love is patient, love is kind. It does not envy, it does not boast, it is not proud,"

The one I've mostly been the target for relates to envy. You see, sometimes when that statement is directed at me, I realize the person saying it may not be aware of how they sound or even why they're saying it.

If it comes through in a sarcastic tone, it automatically causes a bit of anxiety on my part because I feel as if I'm being judged. It feels like I should be ashamed of either my success, good fortune, or something I've been allowed to enjoy. I usually get hit if Paul and I take a vacation or several stay-cations. Most people don't know what we've had to do without, why we need the time away, or even if someone else has paid for our accommodations, etc. They don't know any of that but automatically think that we have tons of money and are living the high life. Not one of them would be able to tell you about the times we could barely keep the lights on or make a car payment. They don't have a clue about the times we had to decide whether we should buy groceries, put gas in the car, or pay for insurance. They don't know and yet it appears they assume everything is okay and we're seriously well off financially. They have no idea that health issues sometimes dictate when we need a moment away. They don't know and honestly, I don't think they care.

I can't say that this is the case for everyone who says it but I do know what it feels like when the words come at me. Has that ever happened to you? Have you ever done that to someone else? Philippians 4:8-11

I recently got word of something really good happening for someone I genuinely love and my heart just melted in gratitude. Is it something I'd like to have happen to me? Sure it is, but I've learned a very valuable lesson. A few actually come to mind. 1) Some things I've experienced had enough pain associated with them that I would never inflict it on someone else; 2) I can and should rejoice when good things happen to any of God's children; 3) Someone else's good fortune does not take away from mine; 4) God has a specific path laid out for me and that will involve things I enjoy as well as things I won't enjoy; 5) My best life is lived when I accept the plans and purpose of God for my life; 6) What God has for me is specifically designed for me – He will get that to me no matter what it takes; 7) I have no need to be jealous of anyone or their blessings because I don't have to walk their path and they don't have to walk mine.

Rejoice and be glad when the blessings of the Lord fall on others. Your time will come.

Pull Over. Let's talk about that.

Do you ever feel jealous? What kinds of things cause jealousy or envy in your life?

Is this something that happens to you on a regular basis? Is there any particular person or anytime where it happens more often than others?

Exactly what thing or things do you find yourself jealous or envious of or over?

When envy or jealousy show up, what is it you do to overcome those feelings?

Romans 12:14-15; 1 Corinthians 12:24-26; Ecclesiastes 3, Galatians 6:10.

If you find yourself in a place or state of jealousy and envy, refer to and study the scriptures. See how God encourages us to 'rejoice with' and be glad for the good things in the lives of others, especially those in the household of Faith. Notice that 'doing good' is more than just an act or action. This should also include an attitude of heart. Is this something that seems difficult for you to work out in your life?

Pray for God to lead you in the direction that will benefit not only you, but the Body of Believers you worship with, family, friends, and anyone you come in contact with. Ask Him for the desire, strength, and courage to stick to His ways. He wants to and His ways are always best. The fact that there is a struggle means you haven't given up. So keep going. God is with you. Write down some victories in this area.

____
____
____
____
____
____

Even during times of struggle, write it down and confess to God what you're feeling. Let Him comfort you as you repeat what His Word says about overcoming, conquering, and being made like Him. Speak His solutions out loud.

____
____
____

How Do You *'Just Say No?'*

Growing up as what is now called a 'baby boomer' was quite the experience. That whole era is sometimes a blur in my mind because it seemed to go by so quickly. The next era was during my child bearing years. My children were born and my marriages took place. As I look back, it seems to have been way too fast and I was way too slow to catch on.My moral compass was lacking. I needed direction. Unfortunately, that compass was being formed within a hotbed of misinformation and unholy examples. Even the people who were telling me to 'be a good girl', 'don't get pregnant', 'stay in school', 'keep your grades up', etc., etc., were sending ***mixed messages***. For the most part, I was hearing one message and observing another. They were **telling** me to just say 'no', but they were **showing** me how to say 'yes' to the illicit and immoral things that this world had to offer.

Instead of demonstrating the discipline needed to walk the straight and narrow, the ones who had the most influence in my life were undisciplined. The ones who could have shown me how it ought to be done were the ones in need of the exact thing I needed. My mentors were having a hard time in their own lives and the lack of discipline was only a symptom of a much deeper problem: Sin.

Oh, Friend, believe me when I tell you that I am keenly aware of what their problem was. I have no doubt that they had to deal with the demons of alcoholism, drug addiction, pornography, illicit sex, promiscuity, eating disorders, abuse of all kinds, abandonment, neglect, failure to protect, and the list goes on. I can tell you that because living in it as a child was one thing but becoming and adult and being faced with it in my own life was a horse of a different color.

For years, it was so easy to point the finger at 'them', lay blame on 'them', accuse and judge 'them'. Then one day, it was my turn. You see, although it really was 'their' job or responsibility to teach me the right way, I was just as guilty as they were once I discovered the error of my ways. Yet, I continued walking down the same path. Even if the name of my sin was different, sounded more sophisticated, more upscale… the severity and seriousness was just as devastating. It was all the same. Sin kills.

It was easy to point out how they had damaged and cheated me. Yet, my sin found me looking in the mirror of my soul and recognizing that my sin was no different from theirs. I was just as guilty and perhaps even more than they had been. Why? I had been convicted by the Word of God and I had gone on to study His Word. I knew better! I knew better but I didn't do better.

I was abandoned and then I abandoned. I was used and then I used. I was deprived and abused then I did the same. I was judged and I judged. I needed someone to properly mentor and teach me and yet I failed to properly mentor and teach others. Refer to Philippians 4:6-9…" [9] *Those things, which ye have both learned, and received, and heard, and seen in me, do: and the God of peace shall be with you.*"

Yes, there are consequences for my sin. I cannot fix the past but I can reach others as I teach them how to say 'NO' to the ravages of sin and 'YES' to Jesus, the Living Lord.

I can also go forward in the wisdom that these experiences + lessons have taught me. I can live a fuller life because I have learned

Ps 119:71

Pull Over. Let's talk about that.

What were the dynamics of your growing up years? Were the adults in your life good examples of how to live as a Christian?

Did you get advice or rules to live by from adults? Were there 'mixed messages'?

Have you had difficulty in sorting out the effect your mentors had on your life?

Have you noticed any similarities in how they lived and how you've chosen to live your life? Do you have a favorite scripture that helps you in that area? What is it?

If any damage was done, did you blame your mentors? If so, do you still blame them?

Have you ever talked to God about this area of your life at all? Have you listened to what He has to say about it? Any scripture that helps you ?

Why is it important to see your mentors as flawed human beings? Are they still alive?

Are there people who could benefit from your testimony of being misguided and finding a way to forgive your mentors?

All My Life I had to Fight

If you've seen the movie, 'The Color Purple', you'll probably recognize this line:

> ***"All my life I had to fight. I had to fight my Daddy. I had to fight my brothers. I had to fight my cousins and my uncles. A girl chile ain't safe in a family of men. But I never thought I'd have to fight in my own house. God knows I loves Harpo. God knows I do. But I'll kill him dead before I lets him beat me."***
>
> *From 'The Color Purple'*

It was hard for me to watch the movie. I found that particular scene to be a riveting, all out 'lemme at him' moment because of my history. Yet, I was eerily captivated. It was as if time stood still and went backwards at the same time. It returned me to childhood memories. It resurrected some unhappy, very painful, and equally shameful adult flashbacks. There was something in the way she said it. There was a resolve in her voice revealing how serious she was. It was a 'pay attention or pay the cost' resolve. I remembered moments like that.

He knew my weaknesses because he had studied me *(or my type)*. He said all of the right words. Things like: 'You don't need to raise those girls by yourself. Why should you work two and three jobs? You need a real man in your life to help you. Why don't you ride down south with me this weekend? You can think about what you're gonna do. All expenses paid and I'll even pay for somebody to watch the kids while we're gone. No strings attached. I just want you to be treated well. This guy doesn't deserve you and you definitely deserve better.' Unfortunately, I listened to his spiel. He was trying to endear me to himself and he did a good job. I went to him like a moth to a flame.

Convinced out of desperation and loneliness, I walked out of my (then) current relationship straight into one that turned out to be my worst nightmare. I gave him everything. I had nothing left and he knew it. He played every card just right and I fell just like a set of dominoes. I felt trapped. Not only was abuse involved but it became a part of my everyday 'normal' life. I learned to walk on eggshells like an expert. I took my kids into that living facsimile of hell on earth and our lives were never the same. It was bad before but this … this was another level of 'bad'.

Sometimes, even now over thirty (30) years later, I wonder how things would have turned out if I'd just made the decision to NOT listen to his reasoning. I wonder how life would have been if I had made different choices? Not only for me but how different would life be for my children? Would I have had the courage to resist the next challenge or would I have caved? It doesn't really matter now because the time has passed and we're living with the decisions I did make.

I wish I could tell you that this was my first encounter with domestic violence or violent men. I'd love to tell you that but it wouldn't be the truth.

To me, the lesson had to be learned that until I changed, I would be attracted to the same types of people and it would lead to my destruction. There's no escaping that I was the common denominator in each situation. They weren't the problem. I was.

Pull Over. Let's talk about that.

Have you ever been duped, fooled, or used by someone? If so, who was it?

Have you ever pushed past conviction to do something you knew was wrong?

Once you acted, how long was it before you realized how serious it was?

Did your actions have negative consequences for other people? Who was it?

If any damage was done, did you blame yourself? If so, do you still blame yourself?

Have you ever talked to God about this area of your life at all? Have you listened to what He has to say about it? Would you consider it conviction or condemnation?

Is the person who wronged you still alive? Is there any unresolved anger on your part?

Would you say you gained or learned anything from this experience? If so, what was it?

Is it something you can share with anyone else as your testimony? Why or why not?

The Dark Magnet

My history is riddled with the 'Bad Boy' type of guys. It's almost as if there's this dark magnet inside of me drawing me to the dark metal inside of them.

There was passion, excitement, intrigue and danger. There was mystery and the kind of things I read about in romance novels and saw in movies...a lot of fiction but I was attracted to it. The models in real life were somewhat similar to those characters except the fictional stuff usually turned out okay. The real life stuff? That's a whole other story.

He was painting a picture of himself that was too good to be true. I felt like I was between a rock and a hard place for choices. I'd packed up a few clothes and left my soon to be ex-husband and moved in with this guy who seemed to be the answer to all of my problems. He had a job and he had a side gig going, his own home, and reliable transportation. To be honest, his physique wasn't bad either.

Yet something was off. I noticed his demeanor changed anytime I even slightly disagreed with him. Simple things like how to clean the kitchen or put away laundry. He never hit me before we got married but there were signs. He'd slam a door and be gone for a few hours and return drunk as a skunk. He'd hit a wall or throw something against a wall. He'd apologize and I'd fluff it off as a personality flaw that could be tweaked once we were married. When we went out, he was extremely jealous and accused me of flirting. Even if it was total strangers or his own friends! For a while, I thought it was cute because I'd never had that kind of attention before, at least not as an adult. *"Oh what a tangled web we weave when first we practice to deceive." Sir Walter Scott*... Looking back, I realize I was deceiving myself. It was obvious that the guy had some emotional and, I believe, mental issues. I ignored the obvious signs because I was embarrassed at having left my husband the way I did.

I felt obligated to marry this guy. I felt I owed him and it (marriage to him) was the only way to redeem myself and find some kind of dignity again. I had left the church. I rejected the efforts from people who cared and tried to reach out in love to help me. Most didn't understand and quite frankly, some had given me unwise advice in my now failed marriage.

I was ashamed, angry and confused. I couldn't face them or anyone from my past except a few family members. So, moving forward, after the divorce was final, in rebellion to God, I foolishly married the guy. That scandalous rebellion cost more than I could ever have imagined. The consequences were not just -mine to bear and that fact does not go away.

Pull over. Let's talk about that.

When faced with the unpleasant truth of past mistakes, how do you respond?

Do you find it difficult to take responsibility for your mistakes? Why or why not?

After you've blown it, is it more difficult for you to face your friends and acquaintances, yourself, or God? Why?

Do you have anyone you feel 'safe' with when you need to discuss a problem or potential problem? If so, will that person be honest with you even if it hurts your feelings?

When you're facing a major decision, how do you process it?

Have you ever studied the life of King David? 2 Samuel 11-12 is about a series of bad decisions the king made. It started out with a lustful look and lingering eyes. Summarize what took place with him, Uriah, and Bathsheba.

Do you think Nathan was afraid to present the message to the king?

If a leader did the same thing today, what would be the appropriate consequences?

Are the rules different for leadership and lay people?

No lingering in the candy store 4 King David — dire consequences ensued

And So It Began...

It was on one of my days off work and we were at home alone. We'd had a few words about some insignificant thing. I went into the bedroom and opened the windows as it was a nice day outside. Opening the window brought a breeze into the room. The wind coming through shut the bathroom door with a sudden loud bang and scared me. Before I could get over the scare of the door shutting, my brand new husband was back in the room using my face, back, ribs and any exposed part of my body for a punching bag. He thought I had slammed the door on purpose out of my 'disrespect' for him. His fists pummeling my body were physically painful but the evil torrent of words he spewed out damaged me in ways I wouldn't have wished on my worst enemy. I don't know if anything can really prepare one for the shock or the feeling of betrayal that comes with domestic violence.

Someone who had been 'the answer' to my problems had now become my most serious problem. The bruises and marks on my neck along with other visible signs of the attacks became commonplace. I began wearing turtle neck tops, scarves, long sleeves, and any clothing that hid evidence of abuse. I started reading up on the behavior. It wasn't pretty and I had a hard time accepting it the facts. My emotional and mental faculties were all over the place. I needed some answers or I was headed for a mental and emotional breakdown or death.

According to the National Center On Domestic and Sexual Violence [Power and Control Wheel/Stages of Violence – originally developed by the Domestic Abuse Intervention Programs Duluth, MN], I was smack dab in the middle of the Cycle of Domestic Violence. There was **tension building,** an **Acute battering episode,** then **the Honeymoon phase.** During the tension building stage, I would do everything I could think of to keep him calm and pleased but it was never enough. Walking around as if on eggshells became my new normal. I could feel the tension building. The beating would eventually occur and each time seemed worse than the last. Afterwards, he'd become sickeningly sweet, even remorseful and fearful that I would leave him. Being in the position I was in, I accepted his apologies yet I began to brace myself for the next episode that was sure to come.

He was that way every time. How I got out of it was nothing less than Divine Intervention and a series of miracles by God. I felt lost and alone with no one I believed could or would help me. My girls had seen things I never intended for them to see. I never intended for them to happen! Growing up I'd made a solemn vow that I wouldn't expose my children to the kind of violence I witnessed growing up.

And yet, here I was in a relationship that was like a mirror image and repeat performance of my childhood. Romans 12:1-2 would have been helpful had I paid attention.

Pull Over. Let's talk about that.

Romans12:1-2 Therefore, I urge you, brothers and sisters, in view of God's mercy, to offer your bodies as a living sacrifice, holy and pleasing to God—this is your true and proper worship. 2 Do not conform to the pattern of this world, but be transformed by the renewing of your mind. Then you will be able to test and approve what God's will is—his good, pleasing and perfect will. (NIV)

In light of the circumstances I had gotten myself into, how do you think the above scripture reference might have been useful?

Why do we need to renew our minds when we come to faith in Christ?

As men and women in the Body of Christ, are we exempt from temptation? What's the difference between us and those who don't know Christ when it comes to temptation?

Is there scripture to back up your belief about temptation? If so, what is it?

Having committed a sin, what does scripture tell us to do? Old and New Testament has scriptures with instructions. List scriptures from both places.

Why is it important to recognize, acknowledge, and turn from sin?

What makes it difficult for you/us to repent?

Why is it easier to blame other people for our sin?

ENCOUNTERS IN THE CORRIDOR OF A MENTAL HEALTH FACILITY

Encounters In The Corridor of a Mental Health Facility

I never thought I'd make it this far. In fact, I was pretty sure that I'd be dead by age 25 or at the most 30 years old. I remember the several really bad habits I was dealing with at the time. Any one of them could have taken me out and I thought that someday they would.

Choosing violent intimate partners was one of those habits.

Attempted suicide was another.

Drinking and driving was the third.

They were all potential tickets to the grave and I have the scars to prove it. I don't say this to brag. It just happens to be my truth. It was of my past and my experience for learning. I was depressed for years and I turned to alcohol to find some relief. The biggest problem with that was that it become my solution to momentarily forgetting the pain for a bit.

I was an emotional wreck. My life was literally spiraling out of control and this was all before I had any children. There were always razors or knife blades in the vicinity. I took to using them on myself whenever I felt lonely, kicked to the curb or was designated second fiddle.

My preteen and teen years were pretty bad. It got worse in my 20's and 30's. My final attempt at it landed me in a mental health ward of a local hospital. Funny things happened. I was introduced to butter on dry bread for a mean. I met a woman who identified as a historic figure from a few centuries ago. I also met a man who thought he was Napoleon. Yeah, another one from the history books.

At that point, my eyes were miraculously opened to the fact that I had absolutely no business being there! It was bizarre as to how much clarity I had in that hallway that day in a mental health ward. I don't know how but somehow I knew in my knower that it was my last time for a suicide attempt.

When I was released, I was still plagued by depression but it was definitely not as severe. I suppose it could be called my epiphany and my wakeup call. My real issue wasn't so much that I wanted to die. It was more of me wanting the pain to stop and the mental anguish to end, cease and desist.

My left arm, the back of both knees and my ankles bear the visible scars from that era. It's not a pretty sight but it's a clear reminder of where I've been and how far

God has brought me. The days and nights of inconsolable, excruciating and unbearable agony have taken their toll but valuable lessons have been learned and I appreciate it.

I was a crushed young girl who grew up to become a broken women. I didn't know how to remedy the situation so, I tried to silence the constant screams of my aching heart.

The list included abusive men, alcohol, suicide attempts – all fruit from the same seeds. Those seeds were planted by satan and his crew of demons. Their intent was to mess me up so badly that I'd miss seeing my girls grow up to become young women. I would never have seen a single grandchild and certainly none of the great grandchildren. BUT GOD! Although I can still remember some of the various violations, betrayals, and lines being crossed, I know that God purposely preserved my life and my mind. He did that for a reason. Nothing wasted. Nothing wasted at all.

Each time a male figure hurt me, it became part of the material that God to use for ministry to others. Those sleepless nights when I was afraid to close my eyes because of the memories that would surface? Those became my journals and my notes of where I had been. The journey was documented. Those journals became my journals of the journey of joy that God was bringing me to. I had no idea that the Lord would do that…*for me!* Those journals, notes and those things that have now become books are being used as words and tools for healing and recovery. That revelation was not just for me but for others as well. Page after page was available to pour over and study for what to do and not to do. The journey isn't just about me. It is about me but other people are involved as well. All knew at the time was a deep level of agonizing pain that seemed to have no end in view.

Over time, I learned how essential it is for me to meet with God. He has slowly but regularly peeled back layer after layer of the damaged, shameful and devastating acts that not only paralyzed my growth. There were things that He exposed and opened up in my heart because it was necessary for healing to take place. There were times when it seemed I was okay but the truth is that I was a storm waiting to happen, a volcano ready to erupt, and a disaster waiting to take place. God and God alone was the only One to handle that state of affairs. Before, during, and after the deeds were done, He was there all of the time.

Some things were done that no child or really any human being should have to endure or have as a memory. They happened and as He exposed them and brought them to the surface, His light brought me out of the darkness. He shined the light of His Word and His great love and I began melting as hot wet tears filled my face for each event. My heart was able to grieve the losses of my childhood that had not been dealt with. It was almost as if a death and burial had taken place and I was finally able to attend the funeral and say goodbye. Some of that stuff was so deeply buried that it has taken years for me to be able to deal with it.

I think the Lord has so designed our brains that it can somehow hide the things that would ordinarily destroy and overwhelm us. Had I recalled all of the atrocities at once, I don't know if I would have survived. As I grieved and acknowledged them as they surfaced, God taught me the significance of forgiveness. Even if they didn't ask for it or acknowledge it, there was a great need for me to forgive them.

I didn't want to forgive them! In fact, to be perfectly honest, I wanted God to hurt them and hurt them bad. I wanted them to suffer a slow, painful, agonizing, and unrelenting torture. I wanted Him to make them pay for what they had done and I was serious. I 'felt' that if I forgave them, it would be letting them off the hook.

Even though some of them were already dead by the time I began remembering, I still wanted revenge. Since the beginning of my healing journey, most of them have died. So, what would be the point of continuing to mull over that pain? The fact is that the real harm would have been to myself and the people that I love most. So, out of obedience to God, I relented and made the decision to forgive them…all of them. Not a single one of them apologized. Well one did mention to me that I wasn't the problem and it was him.

Now, when I say I forgave, please don't misunderstand. The decision was not an easy one because some of these people stole parts of my childhood, broke my heart, and interrupted my growth. In addition to that, I was really messed up for a long time.

So, yes, I made the conscious decision to forgive but it took a considerable amount of time for my emotions to come around to match the decision. I didn't struggle with the decision once I made it. I knew that it was the thing to do. The decision was no longer the problem. My struggle came with how I was still feeling. I always thought forgiveness was a feeling but it is not.

I learned so much from that and it may take a while for my emotions, your emotions to catch up with that conscious and deliberate decision. That's okay because an intentional "YES" to God is more valuable than gold. That obedience to God will come because He loves us, we love Him, and we choose to obey Him because of and out of that love. That's It.

I can't say it was a walk in the park or a leisurely stroll because it was not. I can say that there was an ongoing increased measure of maturity happening for me. Should I say it was an inside job? There was an intimacy with God that I will forever treasure. Those conversations we had made the difference. At this point, I now understand that the person who benefited the most from those times was me. Forgiving them freed me from that prison of hate, broke open the bars of anger to release me into unrestricted freedom in Christ. Those torturous thoughts were gone and I was able to fully love. I learned how to wholly trust in God to the point that I could trust people again. My heart had been heavy for a really long time but when I released my anger, jealousy, suspicion, and hate the tears of love and relief began to flow. I experienced a joy I'd never known before. It was as if a dam had broken loose and the riverbanks were benefiting and swelling from that overflow.

Had that break through not happened; I would never have been able to love my husband the way that I do. I wouldn't have allowed him to get close enough to know me emotionally. I would have been afraid to trust. Chances are, I probably wouldn't be married at all. I don't know about that but I can tell you that this has been and still is an adventure filled with daily choices to either obey God or reject His counsel.

Choosing to obey has brought pain as well as joy. I can't say I would have done it the way He led me, at least not on my own. I would have chosen less pain, fewer things that I call detours. Yet, I know that He knows me and the plan is His and so is my life. How about you? I know that the life lessons were essential and necessary for my walk. There are things that I'm still learning and putting into practice. I intend for that to continue because I want to continue growing, contributing, and sharing what I gain. Every day is an opportunity for growth if I obey. If I rebel, it seems as though I need to take a front row seat in class...again. Nevertheless, I know that whatever path I'm on, He is with me. He has promised that he would never leave me and never forsake me. He doesn't abandon His children.

So, Who Am I, in a few words (The Bio):

I am Olivian Peterson-Brown. Born in the 1950's, raised by a single mother in the south as an agricultural migrant worker. Travel was necessary for my mother to keep us fed with a roof over our heads. This took us (including my younger sister and older brother) all over the north east and back south to Florida following the harvest seasons.

I am a Christian and a teacher of the Gospel. I retired after working in the secular world for over half a century. At the end of 3 failed marriages and other unnamed relationships, I met and married the man of my dreams and then some. My husband, Paul and I have a blended family. That means a mixture comprised of biological children, bonus children, grandchildren; great grandchildren and an eclectic group of much loved other family members. We don't have any children from our union and neither of us is upset about it ☺.

At the release of this book, we've been married for over 29 glorious and wonderfully challenging years. I say challenging because they have been and we try to keep it real. God has proven Himself faithful over and over again as we continue to trust and obey Him.

I am a survivor of domestic violence from previous relationships. After the third divorce, realizing the problem wasn't just "them", I began my journey toward total inner healing. My mission became one to discover who I was in Christ and how to truly be a satisfied, single woman. Initiating a non-angry vow of celibacy, I wrote romance out of my future. After a very successful year of being single, devouring the Word of God, and fellowship with other Believers, I was inspired to write and minister. A lay Ministry, S.W.I.M. (Single Women in Ministry) was birthed. Although that was a fruitful ministry, the time came to lay it to rest and courtship with Paul began resulting in marriage.

Three books (currently finishing the fourth) and countless articles later, the work continues. Paul and I have ministered separately and together as a couple. His love for Jesus, love for the Word, and determination to obey Christ makes our marriage work. We both love Christ more than we love each other and that made it possible to endure, overcome and triumph.

He is a musician, scholar of the Word and I help sometimes with the singing. My desire is to encourage women to recognize and appreciate who they are in Christ. Valuing who they are and allowing Christ to be Lord of their lives will result in better choices.

In addition to this current book, Surviving Stupid, the other book titles are:

Hit Me, Kick Me, Hit Me, Again;

Male Presents, Male Presence;

Black Heritage Series 1, for Apopka and Surrounding Areas

Made in the USA
Middletown, DE
21 January 2021

31879369R00095